SMALL WONDER

For John, our children
and our grandchildren, with all my love.

A dandelion visited by a Hebrew character moth; a large yellow underwing moth & caterpillar; a cream spot tiger moth, a ghost moth & a solitary bee.

FOREWORD BY DAVID BELLAMY

Every day my postbag bulges with letters which contain drawings, accounts of close encounters of the creepy crawly kind and even bits and pieces of dead plants and animals. Each letter ends with a question or questions, what is it? what was it doing? is it rare? and very often, it frightened me – how can I get rid of it?

I always do my best to answer the questions and then recommend a number of books saying 'Please read – the more you know about them the more fascinating and hence less frightening they will be.'

At last there is a single book which I can recommend, for it answers the bulk of these daily questions. SMALL WONDER is aptly named for it lets us all into the secrets of life in our own back yards in a way which will entertain, educate and enthral even the most virulent arachnophobe (spider hater). Written and illustrated from a lifetime of experience and teaching, here is a book for every home and for every school, a resource book overflowing with facts and fascination. I am sure it will become a classic and that many people who have walked in fear will now tread their attics, sheds, garden paths and country lanes in the light of the small wonders without which their world would grind to a halt.

SMALL WONDER

A New Approach to Understanding Nature

MARI FRIEND

Foreword by David Bellamy

'We are part of the earth and it is part of us. The
perfumed flowers are our sisters; the deer, the
horse and the great eagle, these are our brothers.
The rocky crests, the juices in the meadows, the
body heat of the pony, and man – all belong to
the same family.'

Chief Seattle

BLANDFORD

ACKNOWLEDGEMENTS

I would like to thank all the people who have helped me in their various ways. They include Michael Benn of Michael Benn & Associates, for allowing me to use my Gardening for Wildlife poster; Bracken Hall Countryside Centre, Shipley Glen, near Bradford who gave permission for some of my 'story-line' pictures to be published, and to David Bellamy who gave his support.

Brenda Humphries, John Barker and Rod Dawes formerly of Beam Brook Aquatic Nurseries, Newdigate, Surrey and John Gumbrell who now owns Beam Brook, for enabling me to see so many 'little monsters' in close up. Guy and Johnny Yeoman who were in the right place at the right time; Katrina, Marylyn and Munni who were there when I needed confidence.

Last, but by no means least, my family who helped and encouraged me, in this as in all my projects, especially my husband John, who sprinkled commas around my writings in a very liberal way.

First published in the UK in 1991 by Blandford
An Imprint of Cassell
Villiers House
41/47 Strand
LONDON WC2N 5JE

Distributed in Australia by
Capricorn Link (Australia) Pty Ltd
P.O. Box 665, Lane Cove, NSW 2066

British Library Cataloguing in Publication Data
Friend, Mari
    Small wonder: a new approach to understanding nature
    1. Biology
    I.   Title
    574

    ISBN 0-7137-2202-9

Produced and designed by
SAVITRI BOOKS LTD
Southbank House
Suite 106, Black Prince Road
London SE1 7SJ

Art direction and design by Mrinalini Srivastava
Edited by Caroline Taggart

Typeset in Goudy Old Style by Dorchester Typesetting Group Ltd
Reproduced, printed and bound in Hong Kong by Mandarin Offset Ltd

Contents

Preface

Blue tit on elm twig

It is fascinating to watch small animals living their varied life-cycles. Their secret world of courtship, mating, reproduction, growth, hunting and defence is being enacted all the time, almost under our noses. Sometimes their ways are difficult to interpret and need some words of explanation from someone who has watched the whole procedure and who has begun to understand its complexity.

Some years ago, I had a wonderful opportunity to create habitats and to demonstrate the life-cycles of many small creatures. My husband John and I had come to live just outside Bradford in Yorkshire, on the edge of Baildon Moor. Our house overlooked Shipley Glen, a favourite weekend haunt for local people, and in the corner of our garden was a derelict café building which, with the help of the Countryside Commission, we were able to turn into the Bracken Hall Countryside Centre.

We ran the centre for four years, before handing it over to local authority management. The most popular feature was the little wildlife room at the back, where visitors could watch each stage of the life-cycles of insects, amphibians and other water creatures. Both adults and children were fascinated by the revealed secrets of the private lives of animals. So much so that I had a list of people to ring should a dragonfly

nymph decide to shed its skin and become a dragonfly during the night; it was good having companions to share my vigil and my joy at seeing such a wonderful happening.

I also had the opportunity to stress the responsibility we all have towards animals in the wild, and especially towards those we choose to imprison for a while in order to learn about and understand their behaviour. I hope that *Small Wonder* will convey the great wonder I never cease to feel at the way the animals and plants we take for granted behave in their own quiet way. To be able to continue to enjoy the living things around us we must also care for their environment; and throughout these chapters I have tried to show the vulnerability of the many habitats we have around us and for which we are held responsible.

I have written this book mainly with families in mind. On the whole it is for adults who are interested in natural history, and who might like to help children to understand the world around them while learning more themselves. Children can learn to be responsible towards small creatures by looking after a few, with kindness, respect and consideration; at the same time they can experience the pride of achievement gained by releasing the adults or the small offspring they have watched grow from eggs. In many cases it is better to 'look with your eyes and not with your hands', as fingers can pinch unintentionally and most animals prefer to be left alone to get on with their lives.

As you read this book, I hope you will find that your store of knowledge will gradually grow, so that every time you are in the countryside, a town park or your own garden you will have a new experience in discovering nature's secrets.

Networks in Action

Nowadays a great number of words are spoken about ecology, the environment and conservation; if we all matched the words with actions, the world would probably be a better place. We have the capacity to alter the environment in many ways. So we ought to be responsible for all other life and for our planet. But are we? Very often we behave irresponsibly because we don't understand what we are doing or how we are spoiling a delicate balance. Sometimes the irresponsibility stems from greed, a desire for profit *now* which blinds some to thoughts of the future.

About 135 years ago the Suwamish Indians in the north-western territories of the United States faced extinction. The tribe had tried to resist the westward movement of the white settlers who were taking over the land, but the force of the white men was too great for them. The chief of the Suwamish people was a respected elder called Seattle, and, when the tribe was forced into a reservation in 1855, Chief Seattle made some notable statements that were thought to be the meanderings of a senile mind, so they were put away and forgotten for many years.

Coal tit on birch

The deep insights of the wise old chief are no longer thought to be irrelevant. Here are four pertinent quotations.

Chief Seattle said, 'The earth does not belong to man; man belongs to the earth.'

'The earth is our mother. Whatever befalls the earth befalls the sons of the earth.'

'Man did not weave the web of life; he is merely a strand in it. Whatever he does to the strand he does to himself.'

'. . . all things are connected.'

Many things are going wrong on our planet because we have forgotten the ancient wisdom and the natural laws by which man used to live. In this chapter I will try to show you how 'all things are connected'.

Beech leaves

Hazel twig

INTRODUCTION TO ECOLOGY

Ecology is the study of organisms – plants and animals – in relation to each other and their environment.

The environment of any plant or animal is a name for the surroundings in which it lives, grows and develops. The environment is made up of non-living things such as air, water, light and earth; and it is populated by other plants and animals.

The part of the earth and its atmosphere in which plants and animals can live is called the biosphere. The biosphere extends 6,000 metres (20,000 ft) above sea level and 10,000 metres (over 30,000 ft) below; it includes the sediment beneath the deepest oceans and that part of the upper atmosphere in which birds, bats and bacteria fly or float.

Goat willow with honey bees

The biosphere is divided into biomes. These are large areas of the world which have their own particular kind of conditions, and where plants and animals adapted to those special conditions live. The Arctic and Antarctic tundra regions, deserts, grasslands, coral atolls, coniferous, tropical and temperate forests and the seas are all biomes. Each one of these biomes has a particular form of vegetation and an association of animals who have adapted to the local conditions of the area, creating a balanced ecological community.

Each biome contains many habitats. A habitat is a locality with a particular kind of environment which suits a community of plants and animals adapted to those conditions. A plant or animal is at home in its habitat. Here it is able to shelter, find food and raise its young. A seashore, a freshwater pond, a marsh, a woodland edge and a hedgerow are all habitats. A village, town or city is the usual choice of habitat for human animals.

Plants and animals don't live in isolation; they continually influence each other and the non-living things about them. The living and the non-living components work together, exchanging the materials of life and using them over and over again. For example, animals breathe in oxygen and breathe out carbon dioxide; during the hours of daylight, plants take in carbon dioxide and emit oxygen.

A community of plants and animals interacting with one another, plus the environment in which they live and with which they also interact, is called an ecosystem.

The first part of an ecosystem is made up of the non-living substances of the environment: air; water – fresh or salt; soil – acid or alkaline; and rocks. You could think of this as being the stage set on which the living organisms act out their lives. The plant and animal species found in a particular ecosystem will depend very much on their surroundings; if the soil is alkaline (calcareous) it will contain lime, so lime-loving plants such as rock rose, hairy violet and stemless thistle will grow there. Snails will come along to eat those plants because they need calcium to help their shells to grow; glow-worm larvae and thrushes will follow because they enjoy eating snails, and so a community is built up.

Green plants use the sunlight, carbon dioxide and water to produce basic food substances, oxygen and water vapour.

Green plants are tough vegetables; their valuable nutrients are enclosed in cells whose walls are made of cellulose. Only three groups of animals have evolved the means of grinding up plant tissues in order to live on green leaves; these are mammals, molluscs and insects.

Animals who feed on vegetation are called herbivores. Herbivorous mammals include elephants, cows and rabbits: all of them animals with specialist premolar and molar teeth. Herbivorous molluscs include slugs and snails, who, as gardeners will know, possess a very successful rasping organ called a radula. The radula is rather like a serrated conveyor-belt which tears up plant food. Herbivorous insects include locusts and caterpillars whose mouth parts have very sharp edges for cutting into plant leaves.

As herbivores have to eat large amounts of plant food, they spend much of their time feeding. They are the main prey of carnivores, so they have to be very watchful as they feed. Some herbivores rely on great speed as a means of escape from their predators; some are gregarious, trusting in the safety of numbers; some are able to burrow and others are well camouflaged.

Carnivores are predators who eat flesh; they fall into two groups, the hunters and the trappers. It is interesting to see how spiders span these two groups: some spiders actively hunt, others spin webs to trap unsuspecting prey. Carnivores feed at intervals which may be of days or, in the case of some snakes, months. One or more of their senses must be very acute, usually their sight or power of smell; bats have legendary hearing powers. Carnivores have various adaptations to help them catch

Hedge bindweed and honeysuckle

prey, from the high speed and dagger-like teeth of the big cats to the sucker-bearing tentacles of the octopus and the stinging cells of some jellyfish.

Once food has been captured it can be treated in several ways. Most carnivores tear the flesh from the bones and chew it up; if you have a dog or cat you will have seen this in action. The food may be swallowed whole, as a snake or an owl swallows its prey. Alternatively the food may be predigested: glow-worm larvae, the larvae of great diving beetles, spiders and other invertebrates pour digestive enzymes on to their food and imbibe the resulting 'soup'.

Omnivores – including most humans – eat both vegetable matter and flesh, so they are adapted to feeding both as carnivores and as herbivores. These animals spend less time feeding than herbivores but more than carnivores. Foxes and badgers are omnivores; they eat fruits, fungi, invertebrates, amphibians, fish, birds and small mammals. An omnivorous animal has an obvious advantage in having so many alternative food sources, particularly in times of adversity.

Decomposers are very important members of an ecosystem. These are the plants and animals who deal with the waste products and dead bodies of other plants and animals: they include fungi, worms and burying beetles. The decomposers work on these materials, breaking them down into simpler forms, putting them to their own use and releasing important substances into the soil for plants to use again. You can read more about this in Chapter 9, *Winter Survival*, under the heading 'Leaf Fall'.

I have often been asked, 'What use are flies?' Well, among the thousands of fly species, some are herbivores, some are carnivores, and some are parasites, but the majority thrive because of death. So next time you kill a fly, remember – they will get their own back, one day!

The thought of decomposers and their sometimes macabre work often creates a feeling of revulsion. Yet the world would be a disgusting place without them; it would be piled high with dead bodies! The bodies wouldn't even putrefy, as bacteria are important members of the decomposer community. Thanks to the efforts of decomposers, from vultures to flies and bacteria, the huge corpse of an elephant – apart from the skeleton – will be returned to the soil in a matter of months.

About 10,000 years ago, early man lived very much like any other animal. He killed only to eat; he gathered the plants, fruits and seeds that grew around his simple shelter. He didn't change the shape of the countryside

Decomposers at work

Red-eyed adult flesh flies are often found in flowers. Breeding takes place in carrion; the eggs hatch before being laid.

Sexton or burying beetles are mainly dark coloured, but this species has orange bands across its wing covers. Male & female beetles move the soil from under a carcass to bury it; eggs are then laid on to the body.

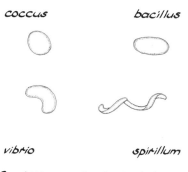

coccus   bacillus

vibrio   spirillum

Bacteria are simple plant-like organisms; all are microscopic. They cause chemical changes in dead material & release food & energy for their own use. Little decay could take place without them.

It is interesting to watch decomposers at work using a dead bird, mouse or vole that a cat or dog has brought in. Put the dead animal under a hedge or in a shady place in the garden; now peg some wire mesh, a fruit net or some plastic pea-netting over the body so that it can't be carried away by a scavenger. Look at the body every day and you will see some of the visitors who come to it – or at least the results of the visit.

Bluebottles are big, buzzing flies. The males sip nectar & the females lay their eggs in carrion.

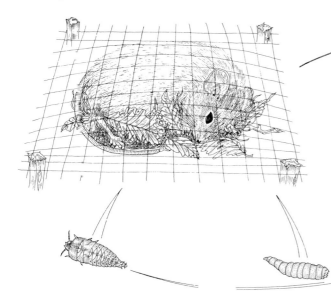

Greenbottles are interested in smelly dustbins & carrion, where the females lay their eggs.

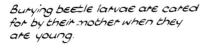

Violet ground beetles have a beautiful metallic sheen. Both adults & larvae are carnivorous. The adult beetles eat larvae that feed on carrion.

Burying beetle larvae are cared for by their mother when they are young.

Fly larvae are legless & move about by wriggling.

The dor beetle is one of the dung beetles. These beetles dig a shaft beneath dung & pull the dung down into it. The female lays her eggs in the dung; both adults & larvae feed on it.

The hyphal threads of fungi draw their food from decaying material. Mushrooms or toadstools, the parts of the plant that grow above ground, carry the spores.

Golden male dung flies swarm around cow pats. Adults prey on other flies that visit the dung; meanwhile their larvae develop in it.

Minotaur beetles have horns. They are found in sandy places where they bury sheep or rabbit droppings on which both adults & larvae feed.

very much at all. Gradually man learned to cultivate the land and to grow crops; in order to do this properly he had to cut down forests to make fields, and the landscape began to look very different.

The extra food produced enabled more people to live and the number of people in the world increased. During the last hundred years or so, man has changed the world at a much more rapid rate, and has become the most dangerous animal in the world. Not dangerous in the way a tiger or a contagious disease can be dangerous, but in a much more sinister way. Man alters the world in ways which cause such a disturbance that it is very difficult or even impossible for other animals to live. To give only one example: cutting down or burning forests deprives many animals – including local humans – of food and shelter. The forest soil may erode and slide into rivers, silting them up and changing their character, having a bad effect on the plant and animal life and the people who live down river. The tree-cutting changes the weather patterns across the globe and deprives people of many natural medicines, dyes and other materials.
It is only by learning more about the balance of nature, that we can begin to understand how to help to stop the untold damage that is taking place in the world *now* and attempt to redress the situation before it is too late.

FOOD CHAINS AND FOOD WEBS

Our lives depend on sunlight and green leaves.

The first living things on dry land were plants. Some left the sea to live in swamps; and from there they moved to drier ground about 400 million years ago.

The light energy that reaches earth from the sun is caught by chlorophyll, an energy-trapping substance found in plants. Chlorophyll is green, which is why so many plants are green; red- or purple-leaved plants, such as copper beech, beetroot and Tradescantia, hide their green colour beneath other pigments. You can read more about leaf colours in Chapter 9, *Winter Survival*.

Plants are able to take carbon dioxide from the atmosphere into their leaves through tiny pores called stomata. Water enters the plant through the roots and reaches every part by a 'pipe system' called xylem tissue. During the daylight hours light falls on the leaves, and the chlorophyll inside the leaf cells captures the light energy and uses it to split the water into its component parts, hydrogen and oxygen. The energy and the

This is a cross section of a leaf. Sunlight falls on the leaf surface; water from the soil is carried to the leaf through the plant's 'plumbing system', the xylem, while carbon dioxide enters and oxygen leaves through tiny pores called stomata.

sunlight

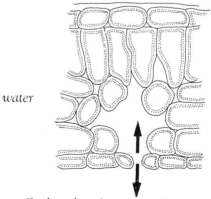

water

Carbon dioxide enters and oxygen is released.

hydrogen are then combined with the carbon dioxide taken from the atmosphere, to make carbohydrates, which are energy-rich foods; the oxygen is released into the atmosphere.

Aquatic plants take in dissolved carbon dioxide from the surrounding water, through the surface of their thin leaves; oxygen is released into the water. So, if you put an aquatic plant into a jar of water in the sunlight, you will be able to watch bubbles of air rise from its leaves.

Animals – including ourselves – are not able to manufacture their own food as plants do, so they must eat plants or other animals who have eaten plants.

Plants are therefore the first link in the food chain; they are the producers. The next link is the consumer. The primary consumers are herbivores; the secondary consumers are carnivores or omnivores, who may in turn be preyed upon by other carnivores.

Plant → herbivore → primary carnivore → secondary carnivore

This nutritional sequence is a food chain which exists in any ecosystem. Each organism in the chain feeds upon and derives energy from the preceding one; it is then consumed by, and provides energy for, the one following. Here are some simple food chains:

grass → zebra → lion
leaf → caterpillar → bird → cat

Think of the ingredients of a dish such as rice pudding:
rice → man
sugar cane → man
grass → cow   man
           ↓   ↗
        milk

The final link in any chain of this sort is formed by the decomposers, who feed on detritus, excrement and carrion – anything that is left over or rejected by other members of the chain. The decomposers produce inorganic material which is used by plants for their growth and development. In this way raw materials are recycled again and again.

Food chains show how food energy is transferred from one living thing to another, starting with a plant and ending with an animal which has no predators relying on it for food.

The first energy level of a food chain has to support all the others, so the producers – plants – must reproduce at the greatest rate in order to maintain their own existence and still provide food for those who follow in the chain.

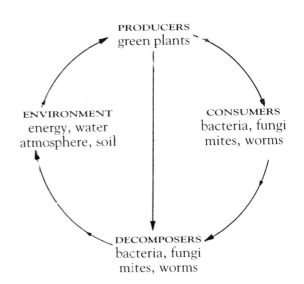

PRODUCERS
green plants

ENVIRONMENT
energy, water
atmosphere, soil

CONSUMERS
bacteria, fungi
mites, worms

DECOMPOSERS
bacteria, fungi
mites, worms

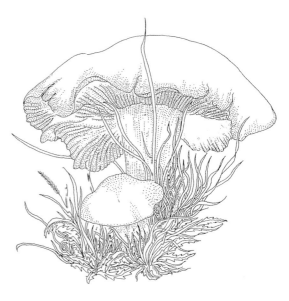

St. George's mushroom

So a pyramid of numbers is formed; those at the base are many, while those at the top are few. The energy converted by the producers is greater than that converted by the first order consumers (herbivores), which is greater than that converted by the second order consumers (carnivores). Energy is lost at each food transfer, so fewer organisms can be supported at each succeeding transfer.

Any serious fluctuations in numbers at any point in the chain will have repercussions affecting all, directly or indirectly. For example: some insects are harmful to crops and so insecticides (or pesticides) are used to spray the fields. Insecticides are chemicals which kill insects; but unfortunately they kill insects indiscriminately – harmful, harmless and beneficial. This means that birds and mammals suffer too. If a song bird eats some of the poisoned insects, it will be weakened and may make an easy meal for a sparrow hawk. A sparrow hawk eats many song birds and song birds eat many more insects, so a great deal of poison becomes concentrated in the body of the sparrow hawk. The hawk may not die, but it *will* be weakened and its eggs will probably be infertile. Pesticide chemicals seep through the soil into rivers and seas, where they kill many other animals and work their way up the food chain as far as human beings.

Using pesticides is one of the many ways in which man upsets the delicate balance between living things and their environment.

HAVE FUN WITH FOOD PYRAMIDS

A food pyramid as a mobile
This is an interesting pastime for children on a rainy afternoon. Think of four or five food chains, all ending with the same predator. You could choose a fox, a stoat, a hawk or even yourself as the top carnivore.

In the picture on the opposite page an owl is the top predator, and the food chains are as follows:

hawthorn berries → wood mouse → owl
dung → dung beetle → owl
blackberries → bank vole → owl
mushroom → slug → ground beetle → owl
leaf litter → earthworm → shrew → owl

When you look at the shape of your pyramid, it may be a good subject for a mobile. You could make one by using a wire coathanger and some black cotton (*see* opposite).

A simple mobile such as this is a good way of explaining to a child how food chains work.

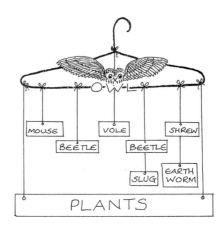

A typical food chain

owl

wood mouse

vole

shrew

ground beetle

dung beetle

hawthorn berries

blackberries

earthworm

slug

leaf litter

mushroom

dung

15

Draw the animals and plants on thick paper or card and cut them out; you could draw on the back of the shapes too, or paint the back of each a different colour, according to their level in the pyramid. The plants could all be drawn in one strip the same width as the coathanger and suspended by a thread at each end; this gives a better balance when you hang the mobile up.

Using a needle, thread a length of cotton through the top of each shape; fasten all the members of each different food chain into one hanging chain. Now, tie all the threads on to the bar of the coathanger, so that the shapes hang at the correct level in the food pyramid.

FOOD WEBS

Food webs are interlinked food chains. The members of a food chain do not often confine themselves to one particular food; usually the range of available plants is sufficient for a herbivore to have a number of food sources, and the herbivore in turn may be preyed upon by several different predators. A bird who comes to your bird table will also hunt along the hedgerow and garden border for fruits, earthworms, spiders and other delicacies. The bird in its turn may be hunted by birds of prey, cats or any other hungry animal that has the opportunity to catch it. The nutritional relationships between these plants and animals constitute a food web. Man must be very careful to avoid upsetting the balance of a food web when he tries to suppress a plant or animal harmful to his economy.

Human populations are limited by the length of the food chains which end with 'man'. The longer the chain, the less energy is derived from it by man, and so fewer people can be fed. The shorter the chain, the more energy is derived from it and the more people can be supported. Bearing this in mind, consider a given area of land; if vegetables were grown on it they would feed more people than if the people ate the animals who would otherwise graze on the land.

soya beans → man
grass → bullock → man

Here is a simple example of nature's balance in food and population. In a wood there was a rabbit warren, where a small number of rabbits lived. The rabbits were preyed upon by stoats, weasels and foxes. One year the weather was very good for plant growth, with plenty of

Feedback interaction between a population of herbivores and a population of carnivores, each of which helps to regulate the numbers of the other.

EQUILIBRIUM LEVEL

H = herbivore
C = carnivore

decrease of **H** ← **H H** → increase of **H**
population   population

decrease in ← **C C** → increase in food
supply of **C**   supply for **C**

decreased ← **H H** → increased
mortality of **H**   mortality of **H**

increase in food   decrease in food
supply for **C**   supply for **C**

decrease in ← **C C** → increase in
C mortality   **C** mortality

Feedback: in living things, and their activities, many processes are being carried out. The processes could conflict but they are arranged in such a way that they work together to produce a harmonious system. This is called feedback control.

sunshine and just enough rain; the population of rabbits rose and rose because there was so much food. The rabbit population grew so large that the plants couldn't reproduce themselves quickly enough to keep up with demand and there was not enough to feed the whole rabbit population well. Some rabbits starved or became diseased, but many were caught by predators, whose numbers began to increase because their food supply was so good. As the number of predators increased, the number of rabbits began to decrease, so the plants began to grow again. But the large number of predators began to be hungry because there were so few rabbits; so some of them too died of starvation, some became diseased and their families became smaller. Fewer rabbits were caught and because fewer rabbits were caught their numbers began to rise . . .

So the interaction between populations of herbivores and carnivores goes on, each regulating the size of the other over a period of time. This cycle can be broken naturally, by adverse weather conditions; or it can be broken by the activities of man.

If you have a garden you may now see how every plant that is introduced to the garden has its potential visitors. The visitors may be pollinators such as bees, hover flies, butterflies or moths; other visitors such as caterpillars enjoy eating the plant's leaves. Then there will be aphids who take the plant's sap, and slugs and snails who secretly nibble.

These flower and leaf visitors attract predators. Among these are ichneumon flies who put their eggs into caterpillars; ladybirds and lace-wings who eat up the aphids at a great rate, and thrushes and hedgehogs who enjoy eating slugs and snails.

The leaf eaters are in great danger from goldcrests, tits and wrens who visit a garden looking for food. These little birds have to watch out, or they become food for hawks, owls or cats. When the flowering plants produce fruits, in come the voles and mice, chimes of goldcrests and flocks of redwings and fieldfares, all collecting autumn's bounty.

These are the networks I aim for in my garden; weaving webs of life among the flower beds, shrubs and fruit trees. The whole concept of creating an ecosystem with a balanced community that you can watch, and be part of, is a fascinating one to follow through in practice.

I hope you can see now how 'all things are connected'. As Chief Seattle said, 'What is man without the beasts? If all the beasts are gone, men would die from great loneliness of spirit, for whatever happens to the beast also happens to man.'

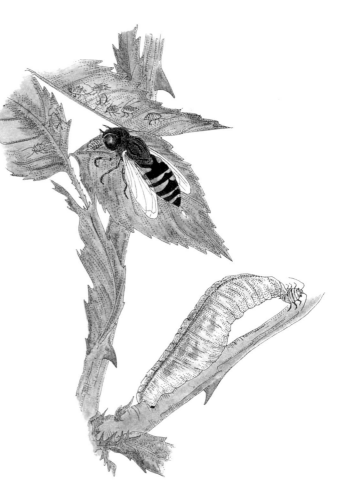

Many species of hover flies have aphid-eating larvae. Adult hover flies feed on pollen, nectar and honey dew, and are flower pollinators.

Eggs are laid close to a colony of aphids so that the blind, legless larvae are surrounded by food.

Flowers & Insects: Interaction

I taught plant classification at Morley College in central London for three years. When the beginning of a new scholastic year came around in September, I wondered what sort of people I would be talking to this time. Among all the new faces there were usually about ten familiar ones. These were people who came to my classes every year, as enthralled as I am by the world of plants and their private lives. I say 'private lives', but really the private parts of plants are their public parts, for flowers are the openly displayed sexual organs of plants.

It was the botanist Linnaeus who first wrote, at length, of the precise method of classifying plants by studying their sexual organs. When the Latin text was translated into English in the Victorian era – shock, horror, what a sensation! In an age of covert promiscuity but overt prudishness, the idea of genteel ladies seeing the sexual parts of flowers was unthinkable, so the direct terminology used to describe the various organs became far removed from the familiar words for the sexual parts of animals. In a flower a filament is roughly equivalent to a penis, a stigma to a vulva, a style is like a vagina, sperm becomes pollen and the womb is an ovule; while the act of copulation in a flower is pollination and impregnation is fertilization.

It would surely be more interesting to teach our children in a way that enabled them to relate the sexual activities of plants to those of animals – simply by watching the flowers and the bees.

Sheep's fescue with bumble bee.
Right: *gorse with solitary bee.*

CLOSE ENCOUNTERS OF THE FLORAL KIND
Pollination and fertilization

Flower parts are carried in whorls or spirals on a receptacle, the expanded end of a flower stalk.

The general flower form – if it is possible to speak of such a thing when so many variations have been played on the same beautiful theme – consists of four structures. The first two structures play an attractant role – they are seductive – while the second two structures are productive.

1. The sepals, which together form the calyx, are often green. They protect the flower whilst it is in bud.
2. The petals, which together make up the corolla, are usually coloured in an eye-catching way.
3. The stamens together form the androecium, the male part of the flower. Each stamen is made up of two parts, a thin stalk (the filament) and an anther which contains the pollen grains.
4. The pistil forms the gynoecium, the female part of the flower, which is usually in the centre. Each pistil has a stigma, a receptive organ, which is often at the end of a stalk called a style. This stems from the ovary or carpel at its base.

Most flowers are hermaphrodite; this means that they have both male and female parts. But there are many flowers that are of a single sex; for example, the hazel has male and female flowers which are separate but are to be found on the same tree. Such plants are said to be monoecious – of one household. Some plants, goat willows for example, have male and female flowers on different trees; they are said to be dioecious – of two households.

Flowers may be produced singly or in groups. The various ways that flowers are grouped together, as well as the structure of the individual flower, are all means by which plants display their sexual organs. Display them they must, for flowering plants have a great problem: ripe pollen has to reach the sticky receptive stigma of a flower of another plant of the same species before fertilization can take place and seed formation begin.

Cross-pollination between different plants is most desirable; but to effect cross-pollination, flowering plants need an agent to transport pollen from plant to plant. Many trees and grasses use the wind as an agent; some water plants use water currents, but most plants use

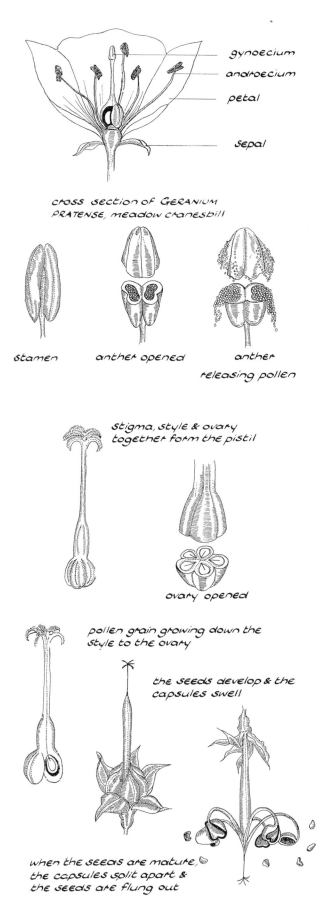

gynoecium
androecium
petal
sepal

CROSS SECTION OF GERANIUM PRATENSE, MEADOW cranesbill

stamen   anther opened   anther releasing pollen

stigma, style & ovary together form the pistil

ovary opened

pollen grain growing down the style to the ovary

the seeds develop & the capsules swell

when the seeds are mature, the capsules split apart & the seeds are flung out animal pollinators – insects, birds, bats and other mammals. There is a bias against flowers pollinating themselves; plants which carry separate male and female flowers clearly reduce the risk, but most hermaphrodite flowers have stamens and stigmas which ripen at different times. In some of these flowers, the stigma is ready to receive pollen before its own stamens are prepared to open, while in others the pollen is shed before the stigma is in a receptive condition.

Flowers must advertise themselves to potential agents; and the most important attraction a flower can offer is food, in the form of nectar and pollen.

On reaching a receptive stigma the pollen grain germinates, producing a pollen tube. The pollen grain grows down the style, carrying with it the two male gametes; when the ovary is reached, one of the male cells fuses with the egg and the other with the endosperm nucleus which provides nourishment for the embryo. Fertilization achieved! But think of this: some seed heads – poppy, for example – have thousands of seeds, and each seed needed its very own pollen grain in order to develop.

You may well ask, what of the pollen grains that land on a stigma of the wrong flower, say of a pansy on a rose? To counteract this, the stigma produces a 'contraceptive' which prevents incompatible pollen grains from developing.

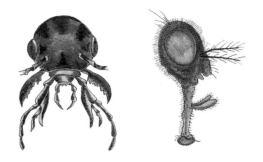

The mouth parts of a beetle and a house fly.

Male mosquitoes sip nectar, while the females drink blood.

INVITATION TO ALL
Pollination by very short-tongued insects

For millions of years before flowers evolved, some plants produced sugary substances very like nectar. Even today a few ferns, including bracken, produce a sort of nectar from glands called extra-floral nectaries; and this is eagerly looked for by many insects. You may have wondered where all the insects came from as you pushed your way through bracken fronds; you had probably disturbed them feasting. (Extra-floral nectaries also occur on the leaf stalks of cherry and passion flowers.)

When flowers evolved, the exudation of surplus sugar led to more widespread production of nectar; this is the most important attraction to many pollinating animals. In many cases the nectaries are openly displayed in easily accessible flowers of shallow shape in apple blossom, for example, and in umbellifer flowers such as cow parsley, rough chervil and coriander.

Not all flowers produce nectar; some produce copious

Hover flies and a solitary wasp take advantage of the readily available nectar.

amounts of pollen to attract pollinating agents. A typical pollen flower exposes its laden anthers to all comers; field poppies are a good example. The poppy opens in the morning and fades in the evening, so it is in a great hurry to be pollinated. Other purely pollen flowers include tulips, wild roses, clematis, wood anemones and grasses, which shed so much pollen that they make life very uncomfortable for many people.

An insect can only reach the pollen or nectar a flower produces if its proboscis, or tongue, is long enough. Beetles have short mouth parts made to bite and chew, not to suck. Many vegetarian beetles chew available pollen in a very messy way and spread it about the floral parts generally, doubtless effecting some degree of pollination.

True flies belong to the order Diptera – two-winged. Their hind wings have been reduced to club-shaped balancing organs called halteres. These can easily be seen through a magnifying glass. All flies feed on liquid, whether it is blood, urine, putrid matter or nectar; but there are four kinds of sucking mouths to be found among the true flies. Three of these consist of piercing and sucking instruments, while the fourth is a fleshy proboscis able to mop up surface liquids. Examples of the three types of piercing and sucking flies are mosquito, stable fly and horse fly; the house fly has a mopping up apparatus.

Many flies visit umbellifer flowers, and these provide one of the best places for insect-spotting. Here sits the male mosquito sipping nectar, while the females drink blood in order to produce fertile eggs. House flies, greenbottles and bluebottles assuage their liking for sweetness; solitary and social wasps, bees, ants and beetles all congregate on the flower head. Bright orange soldier beetles use the flowers as a mating ground and a hunting field, for they are carnivorous beetles who prey on flower-visiting insects. Look out too for green rose-chafer beetles and scarlet cardinal beetles.

Umbellifers are members of the parsley family, Umbelliferae; they are so called because the flowers are borne on rayed umbels. The characteristic umbrella-like flower heads have clusters of small flowers glistening with fully exposed nectar. Some umbellifers are difficult to identify, but the time of their flowering is often used as a rough method of distinguishing one from another.

Cow parsley is the earliest to flower, followed by bur chervil around midsummer. Rough chervil follows within a month, at the same time as the poisonous hemlock with its purple-spotted stems. Upright hedge parsley is the latest of the ferny-leaved hedgerow

The bright green rose chafer beetle has destructive larvae, and the larvae of the cardinal beetle are wood-borers.

Umbelliferous fruits

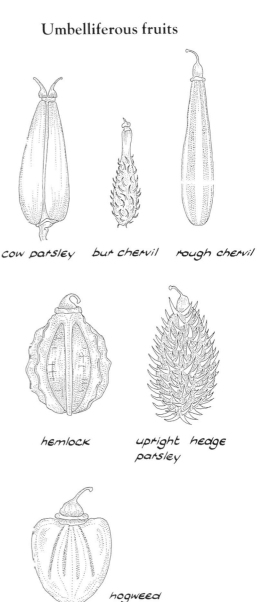

cow parsley   bur chervil   rough chervil

hemlock   upright hedge parsley

hogweed

umbellifers, blooming in late summer. Then there is
hogweed with less divided leaves, which provides
'pea-shooter' stalks. It is easy to identify the plants by
their fruits, which vary according to the species.

*A butterfly tongue is curled like a
watch spring when not in use.*

LONG-TONGUED VISITORS ONLY

Butterflies usually visit flowers which have long, narrow
tubes and flat-topped petals, as they like to sit down to
sip nectar.

The butterfly's tongue is dry, smooth, long and
slender, with fine spines at the tip. It curls up like a
watch spring when not in use. A tongue like this doesn't
retain much pollen to transfer. But it must retain enough
because, in flowers such as buddleia which butterflies
love, the stamens and stigmas are concealed within the
corolla tube, so there is little chance of pollen being
transferred except on the tip of the butterfly's tongue.

The pollen of some flowers is transported on the
butterfly's head and there are many flowers that may be
called 'butterfly' flowers because they are adapted to
these pollinators. These include thyme, thistles, pinks,
red campion and bugle.

*Cornflowers, pinks and campions are
typical 'butterfly' flowers.*

Butterfly 'seasons' are geared to the availability of the
larval food plant rather than to the opening of any
particular flower. So it would seem that butterflies may
have taken over some of the flowers adapted to be
pollinated by long-tongued bees; they probably use the
grooves in the petals to guide their long tongues to the
deep nectaries. Yellow rattle and large-flowered hemp
nettle are examples of flowers with grooved petals.

Butterflies are unique among insects that have been
studied in that some species can see red. If you watch
carefully, you will notice that cabbage white butterflies
prefer red and blue flowers when feeding.

Nectar is probably the butterfly's favourite liquid, but
you may see butterflies sipping plant sap, soft-fruit juices,
urine or the fluid from carrion or excrement. It is difficult
to think of a dainty butterfly drinking anything horrid,
but obviously some prefer a savoury meal to a sweet one!

Some of the flowers visited by butterflies are also
visited by night-flying moths. Moths usually hover before
flowers, stretching out their long proboscis to suck
nectar. The anthers and stigmas of 'moth' flowers project
outwards so they are able to touch the moth's hairy body,
and pollen is transported and deposited in this way.
Hawkmoths are particularly good pollinators.

Look for the silver Y moth on Michaelmas daisies, and

*A white admiral butterfly settles to
feed from a bramble.*

the humming-bird hawkmoth hovering before the trumpet flowers of petunia or probing the depths of red valerian. These are both day-flying moths. The tongue of the silver Y moth is 15 mm (½ in) long and the humming-bird hawkmoth's tongue measures 25–28 mm (about 1 in). Should you be lucky enough to spot a convolvulus hawkmoth, imagine its 65–80 mm (2½–3 in) tongue stretched out.

Most moth flowers are nocturnal; the stamens dehisce (release pollen) and the stigmas are receptive by night. Moth flowers produce a heavy fragrance after dusk; night-scented stock, evening primrose, tobacco plants and honeysuckle are all pale-coloured night flowers. The flowers of rosebay willow herb appear to be adapted for pollination by bees during the day and moths at night. The anthers produce a great deal of pollen during the day and honey bees visit them, collecting laden baskets of purple-blue pollen. In the evening, moths hover before the flat faces of the flowers, feasting on the nectar.

An eyed hawkmoth hovers before a honeysuckle flower to feed.

BEE FLOWERS

Pollen is an important source of food for flower-visiting insects. Pollen grains contain proteins, fats, sugars, vitamins and minerals. So when animals eat pollen they absorb essential materials for growth and repair to their body cells. Bees are the chief collectors of pollen as they feed it to their young.

Wind-dispersed pollen grains have to be small and smooth to remain airborne. Insect-dispersed pollen grains are often spiky or sticky in order to cling more easily to their pollinators; the pollinators are correspondingly hairy.

There are various ways in which bees transport pollen back to their nest or hive. Some, such as one of the solitary bees in the genus *Prosopis*, are shiny, almost hairless bees; they carry pollen mixed with nectar in their crop, then it is regurgitated when they reach the nest. Most species of bees carry pollen on the outside of their bodies, between hairs that are especially adapted for the purpose. Some, such as the leaf-cutter bees, have their undersides densely covered with specialized hairs which curve back stiffly towards their rear ends.

Bees' legs usually have stiff brushes and combs to sweep and rake the pollen grains into place. The most highly developed apparatus for transporting pollen is found on the legs of social bees (see panel opposite).

Nectar is a solution which may contain up to 60%

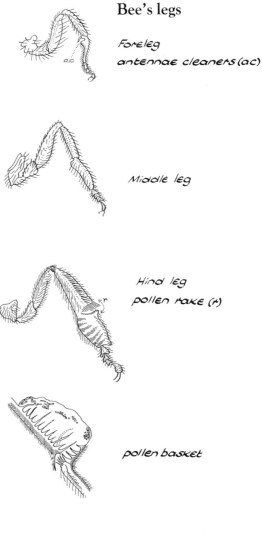

Bee's legs

Foreleg
antennae cleaners (ac)

Middle leg

Hind leg
pollen rake (r)

pollen basket

sugar. It acts as a fuel and provides energy. Honey bees are able to turn nectar into honey by evaporating the water and inverting the sugar with the enzyme invertase. This process is carried out on the tongues of the bees, drop by drop. Imagine all the work that goes into making a pot of honey!

Flowers adapted to pollination by bees open during the day, but within this period the flowers have their own particular 'opening hours'. Broad beans, for example, open first in the afternoon between noon and 2 pm; dandelions open within half an hour of the sun striking them and begin to close three hours later; the common name of *Tragopogon pratensis* is Jack-go-to-bed-at-noon, as this is the time when the flower closes. Many species are so specific in their behaviour that it is possible to work out a floral clock using flower times. Usually this time schedule is geared to the behaviour of bees, who are stimulated to forage mainly in periods of high light intensity.

Bee flowers are found in various shades of blue, purple, red-purple, yellow and orange, which are all within the colour range of bees. Pure red is rare except in poppies; these, together with many white and yellow flowers, reflect ultra violet which is attractive to bees, who do not see the colour red.

Many flowers which look identical to the human eye have varying ultra-violet patterns on them; these are easily seen by bees, who use the patterns as nectar guides. For us there is a great contrast between the bright flowers and the green leaves; if green leaves are photographed using a special lens which shows ultra violet, they appear grey. So bees probably see flowers as coloured mosaic patterns against a grey background.

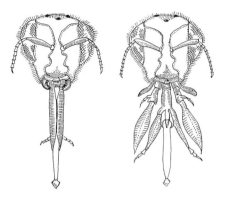

Honey bee mouth parts are adapted for collecting nectar & for building combs.

FOXGLOVES TO FLY TRAPS

In many flowers the anthers and stigmas are arranged so that the flower's own pollen cannot fall on the stigmatic surfaces and cause self-pollination.

Foxglove flowers open from the bottom of the flowering spike upwards; the lowest and oldest flowers are at the female stage, with receptive stigmas and anthers which have shed their pollen. The upper, newly opened

Right. *The owl midge is only one of the minute insects which may become trapped in a cuckoo pint flower.*

24

flowers are at the male stage, having readily available pollen and unreceptive stigmas. Foxgloves are adapted to pollination by bumble bees, who habitually begin at the bottom of the flower spike and work upwards in a spiral, taking nectar from the lower flowers and collecting pollen from the topmost ones. This pollen is then carried to the lower flowers of the next plant which has sticky stigmas to catch it.

The male and female phases of foxgloves are well separated and self-pollination is unlikely; but there are some flowers where it is impossible.

Arum maculatum, cuckoo pint, is constructed to lure and trap small flies such as owl midges. Flowers adapted to pollination by flies usually smell unpleasantly of sweat, urine, excretion or bad meat and they are dull in colour.

The true flowers of the cuckoo pint are hidden from view inside the greenish-yellow spathe which is a modified leaf. Inside the spathe there is a purple or yellow club-like structure called a spadix. Near the base of the spadix you will find a circle of downward-pointing hairs. Below these hairs, tiny male flowers encircle the spadix base; and below these the slightly larger female flowers cluster.

The spadix releases a slight warmth as well as a smell of urine; these two factors attract the midges.

When an owl midge lands on the inner side of the spathe, or spadix, it is probably carrying pollen from another cuckoo pint flower. The spathe walls are slippery with oil droplets and the suckers on the midge's feet can't grip; so the insect falls down through the circle of hairs, past the male flowers, and lands on the female flowers. The midge wanders around the flowers, inadvertently rubbing pollen on to the sticky stigmatic surfaces, but unable to leave the chamber at the base of the spathe because the hairs prevent escape. When the female flowers are pollinated, they exude a drop of nectar which seems to make the midge happy.

During the course of the day the pollinated stigmas wither; when this happens, the anthers open and shower the midge with pollen. When the pollen is shed, the hairs barring the way out wither and the spathe becomes wrinkled and easy to climb. The midge thankfully climbs towards light and freedom – probably to be lured into the next cuckoo pint plant along the hedgerow!

The warming of the spadix and the production of the scent are at their height during the first afternoon and evening that the spathes are open. The number of insects caught inside the floral chamber at this time can be surprisingly.

Why not look and see what you can find?

Gardening for Wildlife

Wall brown butterfly

When I was very small I used to help my father in his garden; and as the years passed, he gave me my own patch to design and work. Gradually, he taught me all he knew, not only how to grow plants and care for them but also to respect the animals who visit a garden – the pollinators, the creatures of the soil and the small animals who feed on the unwanted plant eaters on our behalf.

Gardening is still my favourite occupation and I expect it always will be. But now I look at my garden in a different way: plants are the beginning of a food chain and those chains become food webs, so the flowers I grow are the means of encouraging a certain population into my garden.

Over the years I have become increasingly interested in creating wild gardens, which does *not* mean allowing a 'normal' garden to become a jungle! By creating a controlled environment you can encourage a great variety of wild plants to prosper and provide a safe habitat for animals.

After we moved to our present house, I had the opportunity of converting a mediaeval strip field, which had been used as a paddock for a number of years, into the sort of wild garden that I had always wanted. As I write this, the wild garden is only a year old, but the plants and animals are already settling down very well. The ponds are a home for amphibians, dragonflies, damselflies and a large number of still-water animals. The trees and shrubs encourage birds and insects, while the flowers and grasses bring bees, butterflies and many other insects. Flat stone slabs that once covered the roof of the cottage had been discarded in the garden, so I used them to build a wall with a labyrinth of small spaces and tunnels behind it, in the hope that bees, wasps and small mammals would take up residence. At one end of the wall I built a cave with a narrow winding passage into the garden; to my delight, a hedgehog used it as a hibernation chamber last winter. The garden is a refuge for me, too – a lovely place where I can be content and at peace.

I know that I am very lucky to live where I do, and to have a good-sized garden. But any garden, however small, or lost in the middle of a city, can become a miniature conservation area where a judicious choice of plants, grown without the use of pesticides, insecticides and other chemicals, will attract a good variety of wildlife. The 'garden' may be a window box, a few pots in a back yard, a small patch of soil or a large mature plot. All parts of the garden will provide a desirable residence for many small creatures: a fence, a wall or hedge; a shed, a path or a paved yard, as well as the flower beds, the compost heap and the garden pond.

A town garden or a garden in a new housing estate, where there has been a lot of environmental disturbance, will take longer to become populated, but in time these gardens will have a very similar residential and visiting population to a country garden. I once met a hedgehog who lived in a metre (3 ft) square area in front of a block of flats at Swiss Cottage in London. He had a bivouac of crisp bags, take-away food cartons and old newspapers and seemed content; but no doubt life became better for him when he was taken to live on Hampstead Heath!

A gardener has great control over the residents of a garden, as his choice of decorative plants, edible plants, grasses and hedging will determine which animals the garden will attract and support; these animals may attract others who may, in their turn, be the prey which draws in yet another predator. For example:

plant → greenfly → ladybird
plant → caterpillar → blue tit → owl
plant → snail → thrush → hawk
hawthorn berries → vole → cat

The type of soil in the garden limits the choice of plants. Clay, sandy soil, dry and wet soils, acid and alkaline soils – all these have plants that are adapted to their particular properties. For example viper's bugloss and harebell need a light, well-drained soil; ragged robin and comfrey like a soil that is almost waterlogged. Foxgloves grow in acid soil, while eyebright needs alkaline conditions. Simple soil-testing kits can be bought from garden shops; they give readings on the pH scale. The letters 'pH' stand for potential of hydrogen, which is a measure of the acidity or alkalinity of a solution. The measurement pH7 is neutral; above pH7 indicates alkaline soil and below pH7 indicates acid soil. In Britain most native plants enjoy a slightly acid soil of around pH6; only those species indigenous to limestone and chalk areas, such as wayfaring tree (*Viburnum lantana*), clustered bellflower and bloody cranesbill, need alkaline soils.

The soil can affect the animal visitors to a garden. For example, snails need to eat plants with a certain amount of calcium in their leaves (and therefore in the soil) to build up their shells; gardens without snails may not have hedgehogs or thrushes as regular visitors because they enjoy a tasty morsel of snail. Worms thrive in moist soils; they find life in dry, sandy conditions very difficult as they 'breathe' through the whole of their body surface, which must be kept damp. Blackbirds, thrushes, hedgehogs and moles are less likely to visit gardens with few worms.

All forms of gardening are really a fight against a process called plant succession, which works like this. The only plants able to grow on bare rocks are lichens. Over long periods these plants gradually break up the rock surface; and their remains, together with trapped particles of dust blown in the wind, fill the crevices. Plants such as mosses, ferns or grasses begin to gain a hold. With the further breakdown of the rock and the build-up of humus, larger plants take root; they may be

Apple blossom

27

scrub-forming plants such as bramble and hawthorn. The climax of this process is when trees become dominant and a woodland habitat results.

Most gardeners do not want their lawns and flower beds to become scrubland and forest. So they control their plot of land by introducing plants – garden varieties and sometimes wild flowers too – and encourage them to flourish by careful tending, and the removal of the opportunist plants – weeds – that they don't want to have in the garden. As woodlands, fens, peat bogs, meadowland and other natural habitats are shrinking due to man's pressure on the environment and the demands of intensive agriculture, a wild garden – or a wild area within a standard garden – creates small conservation areas which, to hard-pressed animals, are like oases in a desert.

It is illegal to dig up most wild plants, but some seedsmen now offer a range of wildflower seeds suitable for naturalizing. There are mixtures of seed to suit different situations: seeds for woodland, for damp places, for meadows or for the seaside. Wild flowers spread themselves about very well once they are established, but a wild garden is not a wilderness; a gardener still needs to keep everything in hand. If you prefer the more conventional cottage garden plants rather than their wild cousins, there are many perennial and annual species that attract insects to their flowers. Use the old-fashioned summer bedding plants; the new strains of

Here are some wild flowers whose seeds are widely available from seed merchants. They are very easy to grow, and are interesting to watch while they flower as they attract many pollinators.

Buff tailed bumble bee

The field poppy is an annual plant. Each flower lasts only one day, but there is a great deal of pollen to be collected and various insects visit, particularly bees.

Field pansies are annual plants which sometimes perennate. Look for the nectar guides which lead insects to the centre of the flower. The centre usually has a yellow spot which means 'this way down'.

plants may have more petals and larger flowers, but they have often been developed solely for their appearance and have lost their nectar and perfume, so they do not attract many insects.

The following plants are good candidates for tempting bees, butterflies and hover flies into the garden: all kinds of cotoneaster, borage, comfrey and the many species of campanula; snapdragons, foxgloves, aubrietia, achillea, buddleia, centaurea, catmint (*Nepeta*), coreopsis, cornflower, eryngium, honesty, ice plant (*Sedum speciabile*), Michaelmas daisies, phlox, scabious, sweet rocket and tobacco plants. You will find many more flowers to grow to attract insects if you talk to other gardeners and exchange information.

Among the plants found in a garden there will be many interlopers. These are the weeds, opportunist plants, often brought in on the wind, with a strong capacity for survival. But although most of us have been taught that weeds are ugly and must be removed as soon as they appear, many weeds are really wild flowers, and are the larval foodplants of the butterflies we are eager to coax into the garden. A patch of nettles, for instance, provides food for the caterpillars of the red admiral, small tortoiseshell, comma, peacock and the ruby tiger moth – to name but a few. Ladybirds will visit nettles to hunt for aphids and lay their eggs next to the colonies. Bronzy-green weevils, crickets, scorpion flies, spiders and many others hide among the stinging leaves, eating, being

Common toadflax is a perennial plant. Look at the flower shape. Insects must open the flower 'mouth' to reach the nectar. The lower lip is darker in colour; this tells bees to 'land here'. Watch and see how it works.

Foxgloves and biennials. They are hairy flowers with dark spots which lead bumble bees to the nectar. The flowers are worked by bumble bees in a particular order. Watch and find out which flowers are visited first.

Red and white campion are perennials. They are visited by butterflies, moths, long-tongued bees and hover flies. The flowers are either male of female. Dissect the flowers and find a male – with pollen, and a female, with ovaries. You will find males and females on different plants.

Dame's violets are perennial plants. The flowers are very fragrant in the evening. They are visited by butterflies, moths, long-tongued bees and hoverflies. Watch the seed dispersal mechanism on the right.

eaten or just looking around. But nettles must be controlled. This can be done by cutting the flower heads off and not allowing them to seed, and by digging round the patch to remove some of the roots which will otherwise secretly extend season after season, taking over more ground than you can spare. Do remember not to compost nettle roots, or they will sprout wherever you put compost – with great fervour! At midsummer, half the nettle patch can be cut down to stimulate a new crop of shoots, as many insects prefer to eat the tender shoots.

Dock, sorrel and knotweed are other plants we think of as 'weeds', but they provide food for the caterpillars of small copper and large copper butterflies and of many moths. Plants in the pea family, such as vetches, rest-harrow and trefoil, attract a variety of butterflies and moths to lay eggs on the leaves and bees to pollinate the flowers. These plants have root nodules which are home to bacteria who, with the help of the plant, return nitrogen to the soil, enriching it greatly. Plants in the parsley family attract many insects and their predators to the umbels of flowers; some moths use the plants as larval food.

All these plants will in turn attract sap-sucking bugs, such as aphids, which are eaten by a variety of insects.

Red tailed bumble bee

Harebells are perennial plants; in Scotland they are called bluebells. Hover flies and bees visit the dainty flowers to collect nectar. Notice how the leaf shape changes as the flower stem grows.

Yellow ladybird eggs are laid on a leaf; the larvae are blue-black with characteristic yellow spots.

A PREDATOR AND ITS PREY
Ladybirds and Aphids

Ladybirds are beetles and most of the 45 species found in Britain and northern Europe are predators who feed on aphids, scale insects and other sedentary, thin-skinned invertebrates. Among these the ladybird adults and larvae wander at will, feeding on the creatures that damage plants (*see* opposite).

After mating, the female ladybird lays her eggs on a leaf in the vicinity of a colony of aphids, so the young find food as soon as they hatch. Ladybird eggs look very much like the eggs of cabbage white butterflies at first glance; but look at them through a magnifying glass and you will see that ladybird eggs are yellow and shiny, while cabbage white eggs are yellow and sculptured. Most ladybird larvae are curious blue-black creatures with yellow spots. They consume hundreds of aphids during their three weeks as larvae, then they pupate in a sheltered place on the plant. About six days later the adult ladybird emerges, very pale and soft, before the front wings harden and darken into bright colours.

Not all ladybirds are red with black spots. Some are black with red spots, some yellow or orange with dark spots or splodges. Ladybirds are the gardener's friend as they eat so many plant pests. They, on the other hand, enjoy a natural protection: a reflex bleeding mechanism to alarm and to warn predators. This mechanism also operates if they are roughly handled; the 'bleeding' takes

Pupation occurs in a sheltered part of the plant and lasts about six days.

Beetles have hard front wings called elytra; they protect the beetle from injury and desiccation. The elytra also protect the gauzy hind wings of those beetles who are able to fly.

the form of an unpleasant-smelling, orange-coloured substance which oozes from their joints. Birds do not seem to like the taste of ladybirds and if a bird eats one, by chance or experiment, it rarely repeats the performance.

Ladybirds' favourite prey – the aphid – is a plant bug. There are many species of aphids, the most common being the blackfly and greenfly. Aphids feed by piercing the tissues of a plant with a needle-like mouth part called a proboscis; sap is extracted from the plant by suction.

Examine an aphid under a magnifying glass and you will find a pair of tubes, like car exhausts, projecting from a spot near the end of its abdomen. These tubes exude a waxy substance which covers the aphid's body and probably prevents dehydration.

In late autumn male and female aphids mate. Eggs are laid on to the twigs of trees or shrubs, where they overwinter before hatching into wingless females in the spring. These females in turn give birth to live daughters by a process called parthenogenesis, which means virgin birth – the eggs are not fertilized by a male. Some of the young have wings and are able to fly to other plants, so spreading the population around – a familiar and dreaded sight to a gardener. Each female gives birth to about fifty daughters during her short life, but during October some males are born. Mating then takes place and overwintering eggs are laid. A mild winter ensures a larger population of aphids as well as of their predators.

GROWING FLOWERS TO ATTRACT VISITORS

Flowers provide many opportunities for watching pollinating insects at work. You are able to see how flowers are adapted to cater for the needs of particular insects and how those insects use their chosen flower. I can't think of anything more peaceful than being in a garden in the warm sun with the gentle hum of insects all around. Watching bees quickly and neatly combing their hairs as they take nectar into their crop and cram even more pollen into their already bulging baskets; seeing butterflies stretch their watch-spring coiled tongues, delicately sipping deep-seated nectar, their furry bodies pollen strewn and their large eyes ever watchful; wondering how hover flies ever manage to hover like miniature helicopters, flying backwards and forwards over a flower, wings a blur of movement – all this is an endless source of enjoyment to me.

Some species of bumble bee have tongues which

extend to 13 mm (½ in) so bumble bee flowers have deep nectaries. Often these are in the spurred petals of flowers such as delphinium and columbine. The closed flowers of snapdragon and sweet pea can only be opened by insects with considerable strength and so are adapted to the heavier bumble bees. Watch closely and you may see honey bees feeding from these flowers too. Honey bees collect nectar from flowers whose nectaries are 6 mm (¼ in) deep, or less, as this is as far as their shorter tongues can reach. They tend to collect from one species of flower as long as there is nectar available. Because they are not heavy enough to open the flowers they chew a hole in the base of the nectary and 'steal' the nectar. This does not help the pollination process! I once saw one of my snapdragon plants vibrating and buzzing in an odd way; when I looked at it closely I realized that a bee had been trapped inside one of the flowers. I squeezed the base of the flower to make it open, and out flew a very angry honey bee. I don't know how it had managed to get into the flower, but I do know that it had the impression that I was responsible for its temporary imprisonment!

Opposite *is a picture of an aphid colony feeding on a rose bush. In turn the aphids are being eaten by predators. At the top are a ladybird and its larva; at the bottom a lacewing and its larva; and in the middle a hover fly larva.*

Overleaf *is an identification chart of some animals often found in gardens.*

There are 45 species of ladybird in Britain & Northern Europe; see how many you can find. Here are a few:
1. The 14-spot is yellow & black & not spotted!
2. Typical 10-spot with red & black elytra (wing covers).
3. The black 10-spot has two red marks.
4. The 22-spot is yellow & black.
5. The seven-spot & 6. the eleven spot have red & black elytra.
7. The 24-spot ladybird is orange. Spots may often merge into patterns, so there are plenty of colourful ladybirds to find.

Ladybirds of Britain and Northern Europe

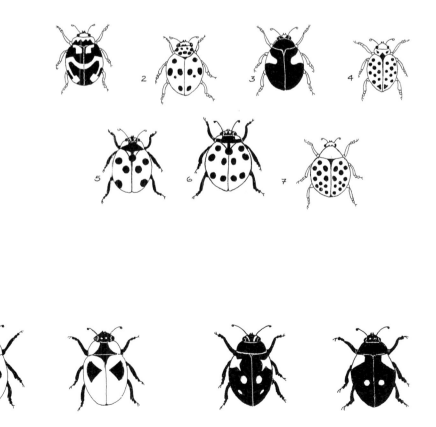

The two-spot ladybird has many pattern forms, the wing covers being coloured from almost all red to almost all black. Here are the four forms most commonly found:
the typical form is red with two black spots; annulata has red elytra with black triangles; the two-spot ladybird with six marks is black & red; as is the two spot ladybird with four marks.

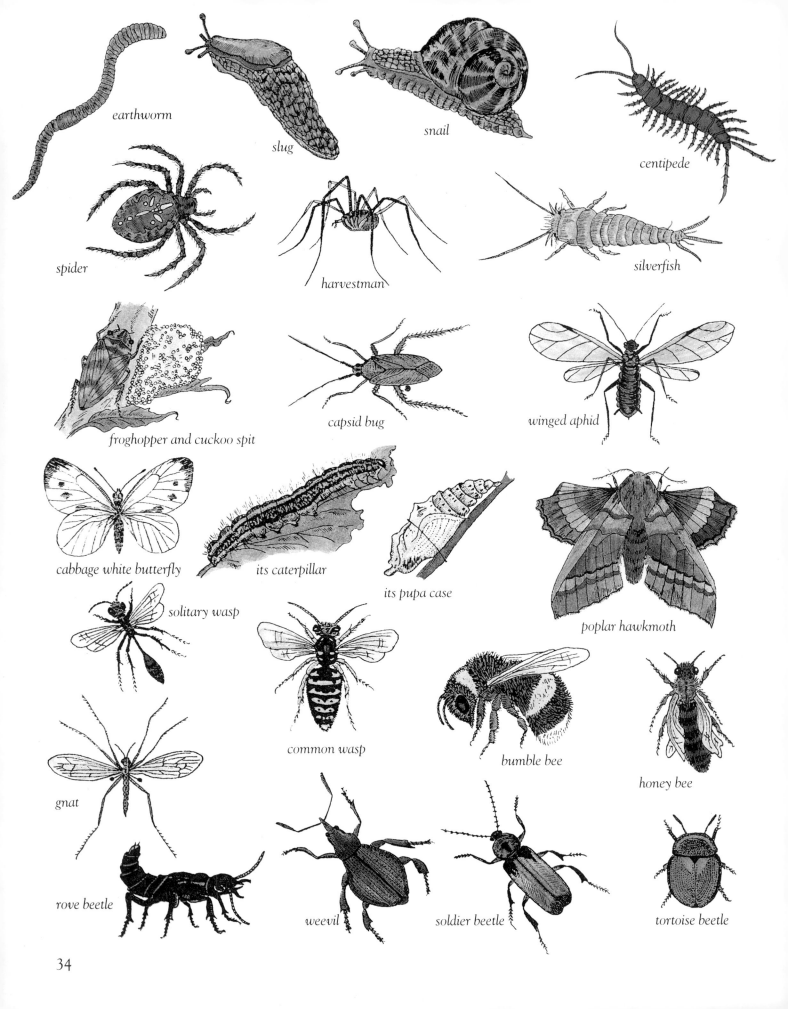

earthworm

slug

snail

centipede

spider

harvestman

silverfish

froghopper and cuckoo spit

capsid bug

winged aphid

cabbage white butterfly

its caterpillar

its pupa case

poplar hawkmoth

solitary wasp

common wasp

bumble bee

honey bee

gnat

rove beetle

weevil

soldier beetle

tortoise beetle

34

millipede playing dead

woodlouse

pill bug curled up

mite

bristletail

grasshopper

earwig

shield bug

white fly

lacewings and eggs

lacewing larva

scorpion fly

its larva

its pupa case

hover fly

house fly

bluebottle larva

ant

ground beetle

its larva

cockchafer beetle

click beetle

ladybird

its larva

burying beetle

35

BUTTERFLIES AND MOTHS

There is no distinct division between butterflies and moths, except that butterflies fly by day. They are some of the most colourful and fascinating visitors to any garden. They all have clubbed antennae and most have bright wings. Butterflies usually fold their wings together when at rest, while moths tend to flatten theirs. Many moths are dull in colour and nocturnal in habit, but there are also those which are bright in colour and which fly by day – burnet moths, for example.

Butterflies and moths undergo four stages of development:

egg → larva → pupa → imago (adult)

When a caterpillar hatches, its first food is often its own egg shell, then it looks for plant food. Usually the eggs will have been laid on or near the specific food of the species. The caterpillar has powerful biting jaws with which it feeds voraciously. The body has three pairs of walking legs and no more than five pairs of clasping legs with hooks, which enable the caterpillar to cling. The segmented body may be covered with hairs, it may have spines, or it may be coloured to camouflage or 'warn' predators.

The caterpillar grows rapidly and as its outer skin does not stretch, it has to be shed; caterpillars usually have five or six instars (phases between each moult). When the caterpillar is fully grown it chooses a suitable site for pupation; some, including many moth caterpillars burrow into the soil or spin a silken cocoon; many butterfly larvae suspend their pupa case from a pad of silk spun on a leaf or twig. The caterpillar sheds its final skin and enters the pupa stage.

The word 'pupa' comes from the Latin for doll or puppet and many moth pupae do indeed look like a doll wrapped in a shawl. 'Chrysalis' is from a Greek word meaning gold and refers to the metallic spots which can be seen on the cases of many pupating butterflies.

The length of the period of pupation varies according to the species and the time of year. One day when the weather is fine and the temperature is right, the adult insect inflates and bursts the pupa case. It climbs out slowly and laboriously; its wings are crumpled and flattened and need to be expanded. This is a very vulnerable time for the insect.

Butterflies and moths have to warm up their flight muscles before take off. Butterflies' wings act as solar panels, which is why few butterflies are seen flying in dull

Red admiral's life cycle

The larvae eat the leaves of nettle and hop.

Elephant hawkmoth life cycle

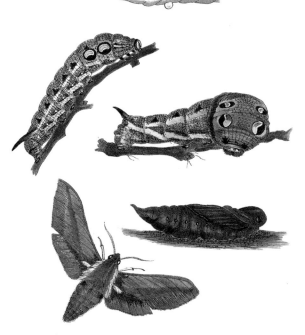

The larval food plants are willow herb, bedstraw and fuchsia. The 'eye spots' may serve to frighten away possible predators.

weather. Moths usually warm up by beating their wings rapidly. Both butterflies and moths couple up their wings on either side of the body so that they beat as one, giving greater strength and lifting power.

For adult butterflies and moths, the main objective in life is reproduction. So males and females of the same species must find each other in order to mate and effect fertilization.

Unfertilized females secrete a characteristic odour from abdominal glands; the substance of this odour is a pheromone, an external chemical message carried on the air. Any males in the area will be led by this scent and locate the virgin female; males emit sexual odours too, but these are released to induce the female to copulate.

During the summer months, specialized sexual display flights often take place, with the male fluttering round the female in a complicated dance. In late summer or early spring there is more urgency to the proceedings and the courtship ritual is abandoned.

The external male reproductive organs are rather like tweezers which grasp the tip of the female's abdomen; pairing takes place in a back-to-back position. During copulation, spermatophores – sacs of sperm – are deposited within a membraneous receptacle inside the female; these provide a sperm bank upon which the female draws to fertilize the eggs as they mature inside her ovaries.

When mating has taken place, the female has to find the caterpillar's food plant; the eggs inside her make her heavy as she flies low over the vegetation. There are tiny sense organs at the tips of her feet which respond only to certain chemicals and confirm that she has chosen the correct plant species on which to lay her eggs.

Keeping caterpillars and being able to release the butterflies and moths they turn into is a fascinating activity. Many species – emperor moths and small tortoiseshell butterflies, for example – are easy to look after. The most important thing to remember is to keep the containers clean, well supplied with fresh food and out of direct sunlight.

Larval cages can be bought, or made, using stiff transparent plastic glued into a cylindrical shape and fitted into the base of a cake tin. Make plenty of small holes in the lid of the cake tin, as this forms the top of the larval cage. Alternatively, the caterpillars can be sleeved on the growing plant by enclosing them in fine muslin or curtain netting; the net and the caterpillars can be moved as the leaves are eaten. Some caterpillars, orange tip and holly blue for example, must be kept individually as they are cannibals, and eat their own kind.

Here is a section from my wild garden. In this small area you will find twenty plants and twenty four animals. Many of the animals are only visitors, but the frog, spider, slug and snails are residents.

Collect some caterpillars in spring, keeping them on the leaves of the food plant on which you found them. It is as well to find out the name of the plant and make sure you have easy access to a supply, as the caterpillars may not eat anything else. There are two ways of keeping the caterpillars fed. You can keep a food plant growing in a pot, although they will strip it rapidly, or you can stand cut pieces of the plant in a jar of water, sealing the neck up with cotton wool to prevent the caterpillars from falling in and drowning.

Put new food in with the old, making sure that the leaves aren't wet. The caterpillars will transfer themselves, or they can be moved gently, using the bristles of a paintbrush. Clean out the droppings regularly as they soon become mouldy.

The caterpillars will stop feeding when they become too fat for their skins; then you may see them wriggle out of their old skins and begin to feed again. When they have changed their skin four or five times, you will probably notice a change of colour; and the caterpillars become restless, walking round and round, looking for a pupation site. Damp soil scattered with dead leaves will provide pupation sites for many moth caterpillars, but emperor moth larvae need twigs, or a good sprig of heather, on which to spin their cocoons. Some butterfly caterpillars may even hang from the lid of the container. Spray the habitat very lightly with tepid water from time to time.

Inside the pupa case the caterpillar turns into an organic soup in which dormant cells, which have been resting in the larval body since it was an embryo, begin to feed and develop. Gradually a new body in a different form is built. Some species which go into pupation late in the summer, will stay that way until the following spring, but with luck you will see an adult emerge and expand its crumpled wings.

Release adult butterflies into the sunshine; sit moths on a shady bush. If the weather is wet offer the insects sugar-water suspended from a twig in a small test-tube. Should you have to handle an adult butterfly or moth, hold it gently by its thorax at the base of its wings – and try not to squeeze!

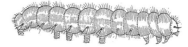

A typical caterpillar. Look for the eyes; there are six ocelli on each side of the head. Ocelli are the simple eyes of insects, & they usually occur in groups of three.

Larval cages can be bought or made; alternatively the caterpillars can be sleeved on the growing plant.

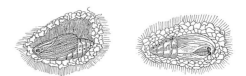

The caterpillars of a grayling butterfly & an oak beauty moth in pupation

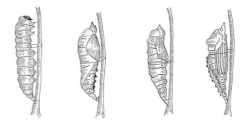

A cabbage white caterpillar going into pupation

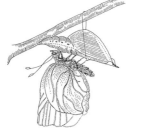

A yellow brimstone butterfly emerging from pupation

A COMPOST HEAP HABITAT
Living in a Dump

In a woodland or on a hedgebank most of the old plant material will be broken down by decomposers. Most land plants contain a supporting material to stiffen their parts, helping them to stand up and hold out their leaves. This is usually either cellulose or lignin. These substances have to be broken down by specialist feeders with enzymes designed to digest tough materials. Bacteria and fungi do this job very well, by pouring enzymes on to their food material and absorbing the digested matter directly into their bodies. This process takes place very quickly in moist conditions, and the resulting raw materials are released into the soil. You can see this in action in a compost heap; the white threads you find are fungal hyphae – the actual basic vegetative structure of fungi. Mushrooms and toadstools are the reproductive parts of the plant which carry the spores. Look for mould fungi on rotting fruit; the spore capsules are tiny black pin heads on delicate stalks. For more details about fungi, see Chapter 8, *Woodland World*.

Bacteria are too tiny to be seen with the naked eye, but if you put your hand into a compost heap you will feel the warmth of the energy that they generate. This warmth makes a compost heap a very attractive place for hibernating hedgehogs and toads. A great variety of tiny creatures live among the compost and leaf litter generally. Some are plant eaters and some are the carnivores who prey on them. A simple way to look at these animals is to put some leaf litter into a fine sieve and shake it hard over a large piece of white paper, a little at a time. Shine a reading lamp on to the paper and use a paint brush to turn over the sieved particles. The animals don't like the light and will scuttle for cover. Pick up the little animals with a paint brush and put them on to a saucer where you can look at them through a magnifying glass.

Several species of earthworm live in the compost heap, pulling down leaves from the surface. Millipedes are vegetarians who browse on the heap; with luck you may find a millipede guarding its nest, a tiny chamber made from its own excrement mixed with saliva.

Ground beetles lay their eggs in the warm compost where the larvae find plenty to eat: they hunt for worms, slugs, snail eggs and fly larvae. Centipedes eat any living creatures they can catch; hunting spiders run down their prey at speed, often impeded by a large cocoon of eggs which are usually carried on the spinnerets.

Harvestmen tiptoe over the surface, taking an all-

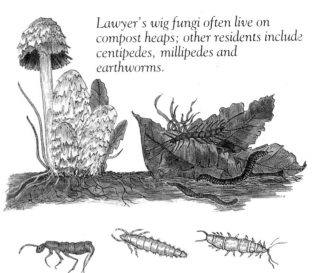

Lawyer's wig fungi often live on compost heaps; other residents include centipedes, millipedes and earthworms.

Springtails, proturans and pauropods are all very small soil animals measuring up to 2 mm ($\frac{1}{12}$in).

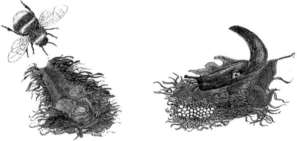

Beetle larvae and garlic glass snails wander through the loose leaves.

Bumble bees often make their nests in compost heaps, and slugs lay their eggs there too; both are taking advantage of the warmth.

Hedgehogs and toads find food around the heap, and its warmth makes a good winter resting place.

round view, as they have eyes set in a turret above the body. These dainty predators snap up any creature they can capture. Slug eggs are often found in a little scooped out hollow in the compost heap. The eggs are white or transparent, 3 mm (⅛ in) in diameter. The time taken for them to hatch depends on the surrounding temperature. Robins are greatly attracted to the invertebrate food on a compost heap and toads will hide in a hole all day to come out hunting at dusk.

Long horned beetle

ATTRACTING VISITORS TO THE GARDEN

Who are the animals who secretly wander around the garden in cover of the night? Many small creatures do not have waterproof skins and they would quickly dry up if they wandered about in the open during the day. You will find that more animals will be on the move on mild, overcast nights than on cold or hot dry nights.

You can get some idea of the variety of nocturnal animals who wander about the garden or along a roadside verge by setting simple traps. Sink jam jars or plastic cartons into the ground with the rim flush with the surface. Site the traps in different locations so there is one in each distinct habitat: in the lawn, in a damp area, near the compost heap, by some logs and under shrubs. Cover each trap with a piece of wood or slate resting on small stones placed on each side of the container – the idea being to allow small creatures in but to keep the rain out. It isn't really necessary to bait the traps but if you do you may attract the species who enjoy cheese, over-ripe fruit or a small piece of meat. Examine the traps each morning and release the little animals when you have counted and identified them.

An upturned plant pot buried in the ground and partly filled with moss and dried grass could induce a bumble bee queen to take it over as a nest site. To make the accommodation even more tempting, put old mouse bedding into the pot – a pet shop will probably give you some if you explain what you want it for. Queen bumble bees usually make their nests in old mouse or vole holes and so they are attracted to the mousey smell. If you are lucky and a bumble bee does settle down in the pot, monitor her comings and goings, noting when the worker bees take over the foraging and watching the numbers grow. In the late autumn you will be able to examine the empty nest.

Solitary bees or wasps may be attracted to use drinking straws fastened under a window sill as a nesting site. Use

Pitfall traps must always be protected from the rain. Examine them often & release the trapped animals.

A queen bumble bee could be encouraged to nest in an upturned plant pot

transparent straws of 6 mm (¼ in) diameter, plug one end of each straw and face each bundle of eight or ten the same way. Tie the bundle together at each end and fasten them under a window sill – out of reach of direct sunlight or the larvae will cook!

Drill holes into a log and slide a test-tube into each hole, open end outwards. If a solitary bee decides to use one as a nesting site you will be able to watch the progress by sliding the tube out when she isn't there.

The easiest way to attract birds is to feed them through the winter, but don't start feeding them unless you mean to go on, because they will come to depend on you. Give them moistened brown bread, unsalted nuts, dried fruit, grated cheese, seeds of all kinds and, very important, water for drinking and bathing.

A bird table can be as basic as an upside-down cake tin nailed to a post. The main thing is to site it in a place where cats can't jump on to it. Many people have difficulties because they are particular as to the kind of bird they want to feed; they may enjoy the acrobatics of tits, the trust of robins or the presence of the quiet dunnock, but they are thwarted by the dominance of squirrels, magpies or starlings. There is little answer to the attention of these intelligent 'intruders'; I think the only thing is to relax and enjoy their antics!

We have squirrels who rush up and down the trees by the side of our garden, but they have never attempted to come on to the bird table. It is large birds who try to dominate: ring doves, magpies and, believe it or not, pheasants. Before we had a bird table with a little roof, the pheasants used to perch on the table, eating all that was there, looking like multi-coloured vultures. Now they pace about underneath, waiting for the smaller birds to knock titbits down to ground level.

Bird boxes must be sited carefully too; they need shade from the sun, shelter from the wind and height to put them out of reach of cats. Squirrels, magpies, crows, jays, great spotted woodpeckers and weasels will get at the eggs and nestlings if they possibly can; avoid nest boxes with a perch outside the entrance hole, and if possible surround the hole with a metal plate. This is about as much as you can do to safeguard your bird box; may good fortune follow your bird families.

Here is a good way of introducing a child to the creepy crawlies in the garden. Cut a potato into two lengthways, and scoop out some of the inside to make two boat shapes. Make an entrance at each end by

Open-fronted 'robin' nest box & a 'tit' nest box.

The guard on this post helps to prevent cats from climbing on to the bird table.

Half coconuts are great favourites.

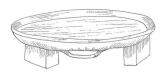

A dustbin lid makes a fine bird bath.

cutting a channel into the side as illustrated below. Now
put the two halves of potato together again, and put it
under the soil with the tunnel entrance at ground level,
leading into the hollowed centre. Who comes to eat the
potato, and who comes to eat the potato eaters?

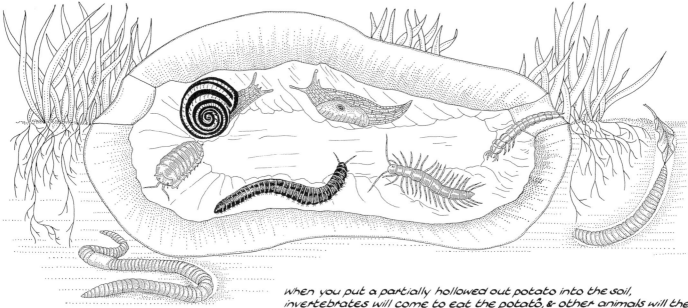

When you put a partially hollowed out potato into the soil,
invertebrates will come to eat the potato, & other animals will then
come to eat the potato eaters. Here you can see a slug, a snail,
a woodlouse & a millipede all eating the potato. The centipede &
the ground beetle larva will eat some of the potato eaters; adult
ground beetles, frogs, toads, moles, shrews & birds will eat the rest.

MAKING A WILD GARDEN

It is very difficult to be specific about how to make a wild
garden. The area set aside varies, as does the soil, the
situation and the time that can be spent on its upkeep;
because a wild garden must still be 'gardened'. But if I tell
you how I created my wild garden, it might give you
some ideas for one of your own.

When we came to live in Derbyshire, in June 1988, I
already had plans for making a wild garden in our field,
which is very long and narrow and is about $\frac{1}{3}$ hectare
(1 acre) in area. For some time, the field had been used
as a paddock, but latterly it had been left to its own
devices, although the grass had been cut once a year.
Having the grass cut down was our first job; a farmer cut
and baled it at the end of June.

I drew a plan of how I wanted the garden to look and
asked a local farmer if he would shape the ponds for me
with his digger. There were to be three ponds, two of
which would be joined by a stream bed; this acts as an
overflow from the top pond, and the water finds its way

Hornbeam

Plan for a wild garden

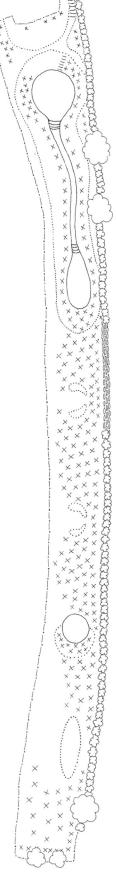

N

220 metres
240 yards

Meadow area planted with wild flowers. The thicket, to one side, acts as a wind break.

The top pond has a thicket at each side & a marsh area at the bottom. Water overflows down steps into the stream bed.

Alder & willow are planted down the sides of the stream bed & these are underplanted with shade loving plants.

The stream bed is stepped down to the middle pond. Hazels & willows grow by this pond which has a thicket of guelder rose, dog rose, blackthorn & hawthorn at its end.

Here is a dry stone wall & the beginning of the woodland area. The top glade has beds for foxgloves, red campion & other glade plants.

The woodland area has oaks, birch, field maple, holly, aspen, rowan, crab apple & wild cherry.

The bottom glade has beds for woodland edge plants.

The woodland area continues; as it nears the pond it is edged with dog roses.

The bottom pond has guelder rose, dog rose, blackthorn & hawthorn planted around the low side.

The woodland area thins out.

The meadow area begins. There is a large bed for meadow flowers.

Key: ---·- = fence
x = new trees & shrubs
&3 = existing trees & shrubs
◌ = field dug over & planted

through the stony bed to the second. One day in July the digger came and I watched with trepidation as the farmer began his work. I've never seen a digger used so delicately; the displaced earth was neatly stacked around the ponds and down the banks of the stream. (It is possible to hire small diggers by the day and do it yourself.) Although I was delighted to see my drawing come to life, I was also filled with a kind of dread – seeing the work in store for me and wondering whether I would ever manage to do it.

Each weekend in August and September, we worked at shaping the ponds and the stream bed. Each pond was dug to a depth of 1.2 metres (4 ft) at one point, so that not all the water would freeze solid in a hard winter. We carved out shelves for plants to sit on, and every root and stone had to be swept out of the prepared areas.

We lined the ponds and the stream bed with pieces of underfelt, old newspapers and flattened boxes, and then the butyl linings were put into place; we bought butyl that is guaranteed for fifteen years. As you can imagine, we had collected a large pile of stones, and I carefully placed these, one by one, on top of the soil which covered the lining of the stream bed. This now simulates a stony bed, with water mint, brooklime and mimulus growing along its length.

Seeds must be scattered over a wide area so that a few seeds at least may find suitable conditions in which to grow. These are only a few examples of the fruits and seed dispersed by the main dispersal agents. If you have difficulty in deciding whether a specimen is a fruit or a seed, remember that a fruit is a seed container and usually has a stalk.

Dispersal by wind: the winged seeds of pine and the fruits of birch, elm and dock have sail-like outgrowths. Dandelion, willow herb and clematis have 'parachutes'.

Wind blows the fruits of poppies (the three at the top), harebell, campanula and snapdragon, scattering the seeds by censer mechanism.

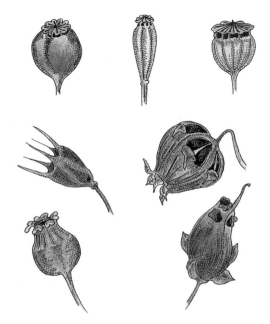

By mid-October the ponds were filled and Canadian pondweed, greater spearwort, water crowfoot, water forget-me-not and water violet were anchored down and beginning to spread.

At the beginning of November the little trees came, and we had a lovely sunny day for planting them out. We had bought trees and shrubs about a metre (3 ft) high and we set them about 2 metres (6 ft 6 in) apart. I intend to manage the woodland area by the coppice and standard method; you can read more about that in Chapter 8, *Woodland World*. Each tree has a plastic rabbit guard and a square of carpet around its base; this is to keep the surrounding soil free from competitive plants until the trees have good strong roots. The trees include sessile oak, birch, field maple, alder, white willow, goat willow, white poplar, crab apple, wild cherry, bird cherry, hawthorn, holly and rowan. The shrubs are planted among the trees and around one side of each pond; they include guelder rose, hazel, dog rose and blackthorn.

It is very important to prepare the areas for wild flowers thoroughly. Fortunately for me, the winter of 1988/89 was mild. I spent long hours moving soil, digging and raking, to prepare the pond and stream sides for planting out the wild flowers that I had started to grow from seed when we came in the summer. I also had

Dispersal by water is uncommon. Air cavities or spongy outgrowths give buoyancy to the fruits and seeds of water lily, marsh cinquefoil, alder and marsh bedstraw.

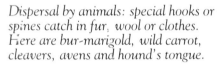

Dispersal by animals: special hooks or spines catch in fur, wool or clothes. Here are bur-marigold, wild carrot, cleavers, avens and hound's tongue.

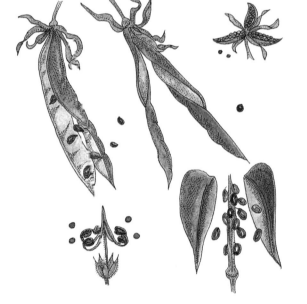

Self-dispersal mechanisms depend on a rapid movement of the fruit wall to throw the seeds out. The examples shown here are lupin, pansy, geranium and shepherd's purse.

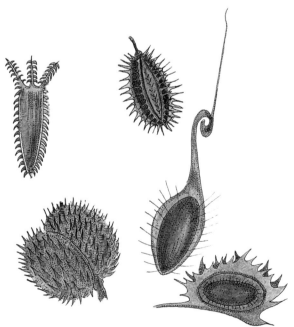

to dig over part of the field for meadow flowers, and there were many docks and nettles to dig out. Yes, I know that they are wild flowers too, but enough is as good as a feast!

In the spring, I planted out wild flowers in large sections, putting 20 or 30 plants in each area. In the border facing south, in full sunshine, I planted sweet rocket, marjoram, burnet, columbine, mallow, teasel, Aaron's rod, St John's wort, ox-eye daisies, bistort and many others. I sowed annuals directly into the ground, and these gave a fine display through the summer; there were cornflowers, corn marigolds, corn poppies, corn cockles and borage, all edged with wild pansies. These flowers have seeded themselves and will be there again in summers to come.

The stream bed is in the shade, with alders and willows lining its banks, so I had to put in plants that are shade tolerant: alkanet, greater and lesser celandine, bluebells, wood anemones, foxglove, red campion, primroses, violets and ferns.

Around the ponds are ragged robin, purple and yellow loosestrife, codlins and cream, meadow sweet, cuckoo flowers, sweet cicely and cotton grass.

In the shallow parts of the ponds there are flowering rush, arrowhead, yellow flag iris, water forget-me-not and reedmace.

My policy is to weed out the plants that I don't want and to encourage the others to cover the ground, making it more difficult for air-borne seeds to root. Wild flowers

Nut-eating animals make stores which they may not find again. Here a jay has dispersed a sweet chestnut, an acorn and a hazel nut. The ant harvests gorse seeds to tap for oil.

Succulent fruits are eaten by birds and mammals, who discard the seeds or excrete them far from the parent plant.

seed profusely, but you can cut off their heads before they seed if you want to restrain them.

In this, my second winter, I have made beds in the glade areas where foxgloves, red and white campion, stitchwort, bluebells, wood sorrel and woundwort will be planted. In the meadow area at the bottom of the garden I have made a large border for meadow cranesbill, harebells, hard heads, field scabious, cowslips and rough mallow. I grew these plants from seed last year, and they are now in pots waiting for the spring to come.

As the trees grow, the tall grasses will grow less well in the shady woodland area. Until then, all the grass will be cut with a scythe and gathered together, as it shouldn't be left where it falls. I find that hedgehogs appreciate the haystacks and use them to sleep in.

A sheet of corrugated roofing material is now almost invisible in the grass; this gives amphibians and reptiles, those 'cold blooded' animals, a warm place to rest. A log pile encourages fungi and beetles, and animals who enjoy the delights of wood boring; spiders and woodlice have a safe refuge there, until the wrens come hunting. There is a pile of rocks too: another hideaway for small animals.

Gardening in the conventional way will not stop, but it will become easier, as plants become established and spread over the soil surface. In the meantime, I thoroughly enjoy my hours working quietly in the wild garden, where I see and hear all sorts of things that give me pleasure.

Goldfinches visit teasel plants too. As they pull at the fruits, others are loosened and scattered. Teasels are easy plants to grow in your garden.

Thistles provide food for the larvae of painted lady butterflies. The plumed fruits blow away in the wind or are eaten by goldfinches.

It is fun to grow sunflowers from seed and watch their germination process. Greenfinches like to pick the seeds.

Natural Builders

I enjoy watching animals of all kinds as they go about their daily routines. The sense of wonder I experience when observing small animals at work is enormous. You have to admire the way that tiny jaws, beaks and limbs ingeniously contrive homes or nests as protection for themselves or their young. Without tools, but with the incentive of the force of life itself, animals build intricate structures of diverse shapes using materials found in the vicinity, or from substances produced within their own bodies – sometimes both. Social bees produce wax, spiders produce silk, while caddis worms and sticklebacks secrete a sticky substance. Others simply dig; but the tunnels or nests excavated are remarkable in relation to the size of the creature digging.

I was once able to watch a harvest mouse constructing a dainty little nest among the tall grasses of a hedgerow. The nest was to be a nursery for her babies and, as you might imagine, four or five tiny energetic mice pushing and shoving each other playfully need to be protected by a well built structure, especially when it is hanging half a metre or so above the ground.

It was a joy to watch the little pregnant mouse sitting on her haunches on a grass stem, holding on with her hind feet and prehensile tail while she used her fore feet and teeth to construct a beautifully woven round nest. The entrance hole was made in the side of the nest and she padded the inside with seed down, flower petals and chewed grass. When the nest was finished it was about 10 cm (4 in) in diameter and had taken around six hours to build; it was supported by grass stem, but it was free to sway in the breeze.

It is necessary to know something about the lives of the builders in order to understand their basic motivations. Sit in the warm sunshine with your ears cocked and your eyes watchful, and see what you can see.

A field poppy has a great deal of pollen and attracts a variety of insects.

A SHORT HARD LIFE: SOLITARY WASPS

Anything you hear about the building behaviour of wasps, bees and ants refers to the female, as the males, apart from mating, don't do anything constructive. Among highly developed insects, the females ensure the survival of their young by building and stocking a shelter. 'Building' may simply mean making a hole in the ground, but the ingenuity of some of these structures is wonderful.

Many wasp species live solitary lives, and although they are common they often remain unnoticed. After mating, the males either die or stay around for a while sipping nectar, while the females work very hard to ensure that the species survives. Solitary wasps feed their larvae on whole insects which are alive but paralyzed by the wasp's sting. Each wasp species specializes in a particular prey, which may be caterpillars, flies, weevils, bees, aphids or spiders.

Many solitary wasps are known as 'digger' wasps because they excavate their nests in light, sandy soil, working with their mouth parts as grabbers and their feet as rakes. Each individual egg has its own nest cavity.

As an example, I will concentrate on the activities of the black and red solitary wasp called *Ammophila pubescens*, which I will call Ammophila for the sake of simplicity. It is about 2 cm (just under an inch) long and likes to dig in sandy soil where pine trees grow.

After mating, Ammophila searches for a nest site, flying low and stopping every now and again to run over the ground and scratch at likely places, until she finds loose sandy soil that is workable. She loosens the soil with her mandibles (mouth parts) and carries a load away, holding it between her forelegs and her thorax (chest). All the soil excavated is carried away like this; by scattering it around she avoids making a heap outside the nest which would advertise her whereabouts to parasites.

Ammophila digs until the shaft is 2 or 3 cm (about an inch) deep with a rounded cell at the bottom, making the nest sock-shaped. She searches about for a pebble or stick which will fit into the opening of the finished shaft, using her open jaws to measure, since this is the span of the mouth of the shaft. She may have to try several plugs before she finds one to fit to her satisfaction. After protecting her nest from unwelcome visitors, Ammophila flies above the site and memorizes the landmarks – maybe a pine cone or a stick close to the nest – then she goes caterpillar hunting. Where there are

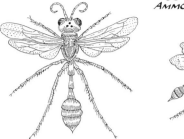

digger wasp, AMMOPHILA PUBESCENS

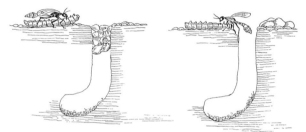

carrying a paralyzed caterpillar back to the nest is hard work

the mouth of the nest shaft has to be unsealed

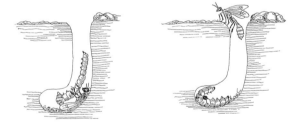

the caterpillar is pulled into the chamber at the end of the shaft

an egg is laid on to the victim

the shaft is resealed

at the end of the visit, the wasp tamps down the sand firmly.

pine trees, she will probably find pine looper or pine beauty caterpillars. Having found her prey, she paralyzes it with her sting and with great effort transports it to her nest; she may be able to fly with it or she may have to drag it part or all of the way. It must be difficult to find the landmarks from ground level having memorized them from the air.

She next has to reopen the shaft and then, creeping backwards, she drags the caterpillar down into the nest where she deposits an egg on it; then she closes the shaft as before and begins to excavate another nest where she lays another egg. She will do this several times.

Ammophila inspects her nests each morning, unsealing each one and sealing it up again. When she sees a larva has hatched, she provides it with more caterpillar food; then when it reaches a certain size, she pops a number of caterpillars into the nest and seals up the shaft with great care for the last time, leaving the larva to pupate and overwinter.

Ammophila keeps up her energy by taking nectar from flowers with shallow nectaries and by licking the body fluids from her caterpillar prey. She appears to spend the hours of darkness among plant stems.

Other solitary wasps nest in holes in dead wood. Look carefully at logs or posts riddled with old beetle holes: you may see several wasp species at work. Mason wasps excavate nests in soft mortar, where three or four chambers are stocked with caterpillars and a single egg is laid in each chamber.

I once watched a solitary wasp bore, stock and lay her eggs in the tops of four canes that were supporting tomatoes. She made more than one cell in each cane, separating them with moistened clay and finally sealing the tops of the canes in the same way.

Solitary potter wasps fashion thumb-nail-sized pots, using clay moistened with water secreted from the stomach. The wasp uses her mouth parts and front legs as tools.

PAPER MAKERS: SOCIAL WASPS

The wasps with whom everyone is familiar are the black and yellow insects with bad tempers and painful stings. These are the social wasps living in annual communities with one fertilized queen who is the mother of them all.

There are seven species of social wasp in the British Isles; these include the hornet, which is a brown and gold wood wasp and is quite uncommon. There are many more wasp species in Europe.

Adult wasps of all species eat only sweet things such as nectar, honeydew and ripe fruit. Wasp larvae eat flesh which has been chewed and softened by the worker

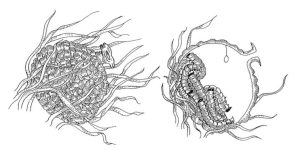

This is another picture of a potter wasp's nest showing the internal cavity in which caterpillars are stored. The egg of the wasp is suspended from a thread.

50

wasps; so wasps of all kinds are useful as scavengers, clearing up small corpses as well as rounding up caterpillar and fly pests to feed to the young.

The life-cycle of the social wasp goes like this.

In early spring, young, fertilized queen wasps emerge from hibernation and look for a suitable nesting site. Common, German and red wasps look for empty mouse holes, convenient lofts and sheds. Norwegian and tree wasps hang their nests from bushes or in the hollows of trees; the hornet uses a tree hole; while the cuckoo wasp puts her eggs into the nest of the red wasp (which is really black and yellow like the others).

The queen wasp gathers building material to build her nest. She looks for the dry, sound wood of fences and trees which she rasps off with very strong jaws. Then she chews it and it mixes with her saliva to form wasp paper. On quiet days in spring it is easy to hear this wasp activity.

Using the damp wasp paper, the queen makes a strong stem. From this, she builds a few cells, her only tools being her mouth parts and her front legs. The queen then begins to lay, fastening an egg into each downward-pointing cell. Before the larvae hatch, the queen surrounds the tiny nest with a protective wasp-paper envelope, leaving only a flight hole at the bottom. When the larvae hatch from the eggs, the queen feeds them on well chewed flesh. About two weeks later each larva spins a silk top to its cell and pupates, soon to emerge as a worker wasp.

Gradually the workers take over the running of the nest, leaving the queen free to continue laying eggs. They enlarge the nest and forage for food for the young, and by late summer there are thousands of wasps in the colony. Larger cells are made at this time, in which males and potential queens are raised; these leave the nest to mate, and the young fertilized queens eat well to prepare for hibernation.

Meanwhile the old queen stops laying, so the workers haven't any work to do. They indulge themselves by eating all the sweet things they can find. This is the time when we find wasps a nuisance.

The old queen slowly dies of starvation and, as the weather gets colder, the rest of the colony dies too, leaving the hibernating queens to start again in spring.

Should you be lucky enough to find an old wasp nest, look at its magnificent architecture and remember the 'tools' the wasps used.

A common wasp queen with the tiny nest she has built.

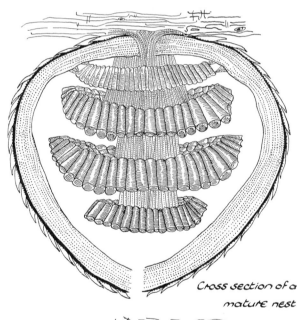

Cross section of a young nest.

Cross section of a mature nest.

In autumn the young fertilized queens find somewhere to hibernate. The rest of the colony dies, & the big old nest is left empty.

INGENIOUS HOMEMAKERS: SOLITARY BEES

All bees are strictly vegetarian, feeding themselves and their young on nectar and pollen. As they fly from flower to flower collecting food, they inadvertently transfer pollen. This brings about pollination and fertilization, and promotes the development of fruits and seeds.

There are many different kinds of bee in Britain and northern Europe. Most of these are solitary bees, comparatively few being social in habit. Some solitary bees are cuckoo bees and put their eggs into other bees' nests; but most solitary bees work very hard to perpetuate their own species.

After mating in spring, the females look for a suitable nesting site; the nests made by solitary bees are very varied. Some look for a hollow stalk or a cavity in wood; some, the mason bees, build into crumbling mortar; others dig burrows into the ground, very like the digger wasps but with more cells to each shaft. However the nests are made or improved upon, the bee uses her mouth parts and front legs as tools.

The food provided for the larvae is a mixture of pollen and nectar, known as 'bee-bread'.

The greatest threat to a brood of solitary bees is the growth of mould. Bees-guard against this in a number of ways. The plasterer bees in the genus *Colletes* are very primitive solitary bees, who do not have pollen baskets on their legs. Nor do they have other special hairs for carrying pollen; instead they swallow the pollen, then regurgitate it, mixed with nectar, into the cells they have prepared for their brood. To prevent this liquid store from seeping away or becoming mouldy, the bees line the nest cavity with an oral secretion which hardens into a waterproof film and protects the contents of the cell.

Some species in the genus *Halictus* are mining bees who build their nests in clay soils. After excavating a group of cells and lining the walls with a secretion, they carefully dig away the clay surrounding the cells, so the cell walls are very thin. Slender clay supports are left all along the passage way which is constructed around the cells and extended into the open air at two points, so providing a ventilation shaft which air-conditions the bees' nest.

The wool-carder bee chooses holes in wood as her nest site. She lines the hole and makes the cells from woolly down stripped from the felty leaves of plants such as *Stachys lanata*. The wool is impregnated with a waterproof secretion and the finished nest looks like a thick woollen cord, with bulges in it at regular intervals where the larvae have formed their cocoons.

Bees in the genus Andrena are mining bees who make their nests in sandy soil. Each female builds a nest with up to six chambers. The bee shows no interest in her brood after provisioning the cells and laying the eggs.

The genus Nomada contains many species of wasp-like bees who put their eggs into the nests of mining bees. Notice their smooth body and legs.

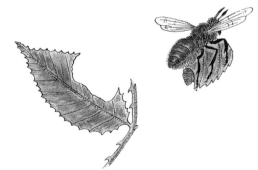

Leaf-cutting bees of the genus Megachile cut neat pieces from rose leaves and use them to construct cells. The bee carries each piece rolled up under her body to her nest site, which may be a hole in a log or a cavity beneath a stone.

Many solitary bees put their eggs into cells that are strung together in a line. The last egg laid is the first to develop and the young bee bites its way out, followed by the others, so that each one has only one wall to bite through (*see opposite*).

BUXOM BUMBLE BEES

Bumble, or humble, bees are the fat friendly bees we notice more than any other as they fly from flower to flower, buzzing loudly.

The buzzing noise is produced by the vibration of the wings, which beat at an amazing rate of 130–240 beats a second, depending on the size of the bee. The larger bumble bees have a slower rate than the smaller ones.

Bumble bee queens come out of hibernation in spring and after feeding on pollen and nectar, they fly low over the ground looking for an empty mouse hole or vole hole in which to make a nest. Most bumble bees use fine grass and moss which they collect and then tease into a hollow ball-like nest in their subterranean chambers, but some, the carder bees, make nests above ground in long grass. They are called 'carder' bees because of their habit of weaving or carding the grass using their legs and mandibles.

Once the nest site has been chosen and made comfortable, the queen makes a thimble-shaped cell of wax. Social bees produce wax secreted from abdominal glands in the form of small flakes, which they then mould into shape. The wax cell is stocked with 'bee-bread' on to which the queen lays about ten of the eggs which have developed inside her body since her autumn mating; then she seals the top of the pot up with a wax lid. The queen makes another cell, a honey pot, which contains nectar and pollen; these are provisions for cold rainy days when she can't go out to collect food. She incubates her eggs with the warmth of her body and, when the larvae hatch, opens the lid of their cell from time to time to give them more food.

Two or three weeks after the eggs were laid, the first little bumble bees emerge. They are only small because they have been cramped into a small space and not very well fed, but as the season advances the bumble bees that emerge get progressively larger, having been better supplied with food and living space.

While the queen lays eggs, her daughters work hard, foraging for food, enlarging and defending the nest and building new cells. The colony grows until there are

The leaf-cutting bee twists the leaf ovals into a thimble-shaped cell which she stocks with bee-bread, then she lays an egg on to the food. The next piece she cuts is circular, and this makes the lid of one cell and the back wall of the next.

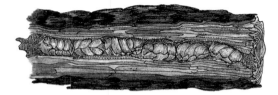

Beginning a bumble bee colony

The queen bumble bee makes a hollow ball-like nest of grass & moss.

The queen makes a cell & stocks it with pollen, on which she lays her eggs; then she makes a honey pot which is filled with nectar for rainy days.

several hundred bumble bees hard at work, but by this time summer is near its end and the queen lays both fertilized and unfertilized eggs. Larvae from the fertilized eggs laid at this time of year are fed a great deal of food and the extra nourishment enables them to become queens. The unfertilized eggs become drones, male bees.

The young queens and males disperse and mate with bees from other colonies. By late autumn the old queen, the workers and the drones have all died of cold and starvation, and the young queens, now fertilized, find a sheltered place where they overwinter.

I watched this process for the first time when someone gave me an old rug in the folds of which a buff-tailed bumble bee queen had just started her nest. I only looked when she had gone out foraging, and I left the nest alone as soon as the first brood emerged. In autumn it was surprising to see how many cells had been constructed and how neat the nest was.

The queen incubates the eggs by sitting on the cell to keep it warm, only leaving the nest to feed.

As the larvae grow, the walls of the cell bulge outwards. When fully developed, each larva spins a cocoon in which she pupates.

The empty cocoons are not used again for eggs but they are used as storage jars. New cells, bulging & irregular, are built on empty cocoons.

A HOME MADE FROM WAX: HONEY BEES

There are between 20,000 and 80,000 individuals in a strong colony of honey bees. All these bees are the offspring of one queen who is a highly developed egg-laying machine, playing no other active part in the economy of the hive. The queen honey bee usually lives for several years whereas the drones, who are all males, and summer workers are short-lived.

During the spring and summer, the colony contains a number of drones; these are large, stingless bees whose sole function in life is to mate with any virgin queen they find whilst out flying in the sunshine. Having mated they die. If they are still in the hive in the autumn they are usually killed or turned out by the worker bees.

The vast majority of honey bees are workers. These are infertile females capable of performing all the routine jobs of the hive. The worker bees do not have specialist jobs; rather their job changes with their age because they are capable of doing certain jobs at certain stages of development. For example, young bees produce royal jelly. This is fed to larvae for three days after they hatch. Thereafter, most larvae are fed on pollen and honey, but a larva chosen to become a queen is always fed on royal jelly. When the glands which produce this protein-rich jelly dry up, the wax glands come into action and the worker bee becomes a builder; at the third stage of her development she becomes a forager. Throughout these stages the worker is also carrying out other work in the hive.

Inside a beehive

Honey bees are perennial, & make long-lasting wax combs. Wax is a fatty substance produced by glands in the bee's abdomen, & secreted from between the body segments in the form of flakes.

In contrast to the paper nests of social wasps, with their downward-facing cells, the combs of honey bees are made of wax. The combs hang vertically and have cells on each side, separated by a thin wall in the middle. The wax cells of the honey bee are used for rearing the brood and to store pollen and nectar.

A piece of comb measuring 37 by 22.5 cm (15 by 9 in) can hold more than 2 kg (4–4½ lbs) of honey, yet in the manufacture of the comb the bees use only about 40 gm (1½ oz) of wax. Each cell is a hexagon – a very economical shape which is space-saving and very strong, using far less wax than any other shape of the same area. Cells are usually built with one corner of the hexagonal prism pointing to the top and another to the ground; the skill of their builders is remarkable.

The cell walls are built with a gradient of 13° from base to opening, enough to prevent the nectar or honey from running out. The distance from one cell wall to the opposite wall is 5.2 mm in a worker cell and 6.2 mm in a drone cell, because drones are larger than workers. The thickness of each cell wall is 0.073 mm.

How do bees measure with such precision?

The bee uses its own head as a plumb bob to determine the line of gravity; the size of each cell is measured with the tips of the front legs, and the thickness of the cell walls is determined by sense organs on the tips of the antennae.

When we had our Countryside Centre, I had an observation beehive; and so I was able to watch honey bees to my heart's content as well as to experiment with the behavioural activities of the bees. For example, I took the queen bee out of the observation hive so we could see how she was replaced. The bees fed one of the female grubs on royal jelly until its pupation time arrived and the extra large grub became the next queen. We set out coloured cards, each with a tiny saucer of honey, to see which colours the bees preferred. We marked bees while they were gathering pollen and watched the dance they performed when they returned to the hive. This proved the accuracy of the bee dances. My experiments were always kind and never harmed the bees.

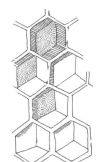

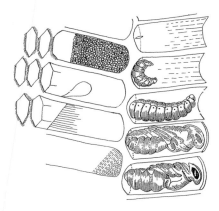

The cells are built with a 13° gradient from base to opening, to prevent the honey from running out. The cells are used to store pollen, nectar & honey; sometimes water & propolis are stored. The cells in the centre of the comb are used for the brood.

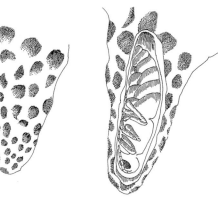

A queen honey bee never founds a colony on her own. Worker bees raise new queens by feeding a few female larvae on special food. Queen cells are larger than other cells & hang down.

SILK SPINNERS: ORB WEB SPIDERS

The largest of the traditional cartwheel cobwebs are made by the garden cross or diadem spider, *Araneus diadematus*, one of the many species of orb web spiders.

All spiders produce silk, which is manufactured in glands installed in the spider's abdomen. There are usually six pairs of glands, each producing its own type of thread, so that dry threads, sticky threads, fine threads, threads for enveloping eggs and threads for securing prey can all be produced by the spider at will.

Imagine that the spider is sitting on a firm twig to make the hanging web. It will first have to make a bridge between the twig and another solid object; to do this, it lifts its abdomen, stretches the movable spinneret nozzles as far apart as they will go and produces two short threads; then it inclines the spinnerets together so that when the threads emerge they combine into one strand. This results in the production of a tiny kite which will float on an air current and fasten itself to a firm object, taking the main thread with it.

The spider tests the strength of the bridge thoroughly by tugging at it and walking across it a few times. It begins to cross the bridge in an odd way: it bites the thread but keeps hold of both bitten ends; then, running forward with its body between them, it shoots out a new thread from behind and rolls up the thread that is in front. Because more thread is produced than is rolled up, the bridge begins to sag and at the halfway point the spider sticks the two ends together and drops downwards. On reaching a firm landing stage, the spider takes a few steps sideways to incline the web, and then secures it. The first three spokes are completed.

The next movements are very fast as the spider runs backwards and forwards, to the hub from the rim, spinning the dry framework of the web. Now the web is ready for the spirals. The first few spirals around the hub create a strengthening zone of dry threads; but from there to the rim extends the sticky trapping zone. The silk in this zone is coated with gum exuded by the spider, which often shows as beads on the spirals. The spider avoids sticking to its own web by coating its feet with oil and using the dry spokes wherever possible.

During the day the sticky threads have to be renewed; the web is repaired after victims have been snared and the whole web is remade every few days.

The spider often sits in the centre of the web; but a little hideout at its edge serves as a shelter at night and in bad weather. Many species of spider keep two legs on a signal strand. This strand runs from the retreat to the

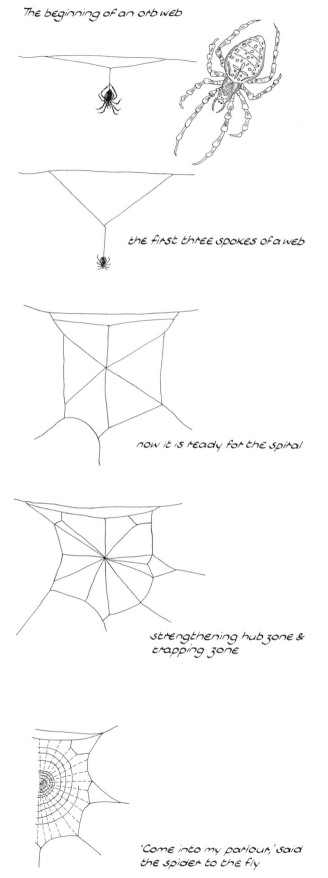

The beginning of an orb web

the first three spokes of a web

now it is ready for the spiral

strengthening hub zone & trapping zone

'Come into my parlour,' said the spider to the fly

hub and advises the waiting spider that a victim is struggling in the web.

An average orb web has over a thousand junctions which unite about 20 metres (65 ft) of silk; this weighs less than half a milligramme (1/50,000 oz). Yet some of the orb web spinners are among our largest and heaviest spiders – a female garden cross spider may well weigh 2.25 gm ($^1/_{12}$ oz).

It is easy to watch a spider spin a web. Use a large covered see-through container and put a loose arrangement of twigs inside. Gently and carefully introduce a spider and watch patiently. When the web is complete, put one or two live flies into the container and watch how the spider captures its prey. Put the spider back outside after a day or so.

INVENTORS OF THE DIVING BELL
Water Spiders

Raft spiders and pirate wolf spiders live and hunt in marshy areas and around woodland ponds, but the water spider *Argyroneta aquatica* is unique: it is the only known spider in the world that lives mostly under water. Water spiders live in deep, unpolluted water and there are thriving populations in some parts of the British Isles and northern Europe.

The spiders are dark brown with long, strong, hairy legs. It is unusual for male spiders to be larger than the females; but the male water spider has a body measuring about 13 mm ($^1/_2$ in) while an adult female is only about 10 mm ($^3/_8$ in) long.

Though they do show cannibalistic tendencies when in groups, a pair will live happily in a covered aquarium. I am very fond of water spiders and I've spent many hours watching them getting on with their lives.

Although the spider lives under water, it still breathes air from the atmosphere. When a water spider moves around in the water, the whole of its abdomen appears to be silver, because of the air trapped amongst the fine velvety hairs of its body. The trapped air supplies the spider with oxygen for some time, but when it needs replenishing the spider rises to the water surface, sticks its back end out of the water and so renews its bubble of air. But the spider needs an operational centre in which it can feed, and so it builds an air-filled shelter of silk under the water amongst the plants.

A fine silken web is spun among the water plants and anchored firmly. Then the spider makes several journeys

water spiders in action

to the water surface, each time carrying back a large bubble of air trapped between its back legs and abdomen. The bubble is released under the web by stroking actions of the legs; the air raises the web, pushing it up and expanding it. As the web fills and rises, a bell-shaped construction is formed. The oxygen inside the diving bell is used up very slowly. As it is used, carbon dioxide is released into the surrounding water; at the same time oxygen from the water diffuses into the spider's diving bell, making it a very efficient oxygen tent. If the surrounding water becomes warm and therefore short of oxygen, the spider carries air from the bell and releases it at the water surface, carrying a fresh bubble down to replace the old.

Lines of silk are spun among the plants, and these vibrate when food is around; so tadpoles, fish fry, daphnia and midge larvae all fall prey to the spider, who carries the victim back to the bell to suck out the juices.

Late spring is the time for reproduction; I have watched a male water spider catch a tadpole and offer it to a female as she came out of her diving bell. She accepted the tadpole and the male popped his sperm-laden palp into the female's vagina while she was eating the tadpole within the safety of her diving bell, seemingly oblivious of his attentions.

After mating, the female spins an egg sac of dense silk at the top of her diving bell. She lays between 50 and 100 eggs, which she actively and fiercely guards; after about three weeks the eggs hatch and the mother spider provides food for her spiderlings for two weeks or more. Then, one day, many minute silver bubbles appear in the water; and on close inspection tiny spiders can be seen, each with its own air bubble.

The spiderlings are too small to make diving bells, so they live in empty snail shells or in cavities between stones until they grow bigger.

CASE CONSTRUCTIONS: CADDIS FLIES

Caddis flies flit around waterside vegetation at dusk and they hide by day. They have two pairs of grey-brown wings which are covered with fine hairs; these wings are held tent-like above the body when the insect is at rest. They spend the greater part of their lives under water in the larval state and they are easily found and recognized in freshwater habitats.

Watching caddis 'worms' is fascinating. The tube-building species are easy to care for as they feed on algae

Adult caddis fly with eggs

and fresh or decaying plant material. You can watch the whole life-cycle by starting with the eggs, which are laid on plant stems in a curved mass of jelly.

The larvae are soft and caterpillar-like when they emerge from the eggs. Almost as soon as they hatch they begin to spin little tubes about themselves, using silk produced from the salivary glands. The silk tube has to be strengthened; each species favours different building materials and arranges them in a characteristic way. Bits of vegetation, grains of sand, tiny pebbles, minuscule snail shells or twigs are fastened on to the silken tube. Some arrange the building materials in a spiral; some are haphazard in their method; some use two materials, for example sand grains and pieces of small twigs. The favoured material may not be available and so the larvae may have to use whatever they find within their habitat, but the casings built will blend in with the environment and successfully camouflage their owners.

Light materials are usually used in still water, but in moving water, where a little weight acts as an anchor, heavier materials are attached to the silken tube.

This building behaviour pattern is fascinating, and I have found it easy to persuade the caddis worms to make tubes decorated with materials supplied, simply by ensuring they are the only ones available. Coloured beads, non-sharp bits of glass or tiny bits of pottery are possibilities. Of course, these decorative caddis worms have to be cared for until after pupation, as they would very soon be spotted by a predator if they were put back into the wild.

The larva is firmly attached to its case by a pair of hooks situated at the tip of its abdomen. Feathery gills undulate inside the case so that water passes over the body constantly, enabling the larva to extract the oxygen.

The caddis worm in its tube slowly meanders over the vegetation, pulling itself along by its protruding legs and withdrawing completely into the tube when disturbed. The tube has to be enlarged as the larva grows, and when it is fully grown the tube is anchored to a stone or a plant by silken threads and the entrance is fastened with a fine silken membrane; then pupation begins.

Net-building caddis worms don't make a protective case; they are carnivorous and live in fast-flowing streams where they can position their fishing nets so that the current carries small animals into the open end. The larva sits in its net and snaps up the captured prey as it arrives. When these larvae pupate, they spin a silk cocoon in a sandy chamber or under a stone, rising to the surface for the adult to emerge.

Sand grain case made by POTAMOPHYLAX species

LIMNEPHILUS FLAVICORNIS makes a case of tiny shells.

Other LIMNEPHILUS species use plant material to make cases.

Caddis flies in the genus HYDROPSYCHE are found in fast-flowing streams, where the larvae live in silken nets.

Many caddis flies emerge in late spring and early summer for a very short adult life. They dance over the water surface on warm evenings in little swarms, easy prey for bats and birds.

Oddly enough, there are some very small moths whose caterpillars make a tube as camouflage, in the same way as caddis worms. These caterpillars are called bagworms and are the larval stage of moths in the family Psychidae.

The female moths are wingless and sit on the trunks of trees waiting for the males to 'smell them out' and mate with them. Eggs are laid on the bark and, when the tiny caterpillars hatch, they spin little tubes of silk around their soft bodies. The camouflage material is composed of soil particles or small bits of plant attached to the tube. Like the caddis worms, bagworms never leave their protective tubes until they emerge as adults. They graze on moss and lichen, well camouflaged from the sharp eyes of birds and the curious eyes of naturalists!

ONE PARENT FAMILY
Three-Spined Stickleback

The three-spined stickleback is a lively little fish which grows to a length of 9 cm (3½ in). Its dorsal fins consist of three separate stiff spines which are raised in fear or aggression. The body does not have scales; instead it has an armour of bony plates.

In spring, the male stickleback develops his breeding colours; his throat and belly become red, the eyes blue and the back a shimmering blue-green. Each male isolates himself and selects a territory which he defends fiercely. He excavates a saucer-shaped depression by sucking mouthfuls of sand or silt from the bottom of his pond or stream habitat and spitting it out away from the site. Then he gathers bits of pond weed from around his territory and puts them into the depression; he sticks them together with a kidney secretion which is released when he presses himself against the gathered vegetation. After much gathering, packing and gluing, the nest mound is ready and the male wriggles into it to make a tunnel through the middle.

Meanwhile the female sticklebacks, heavy with eggs, become interested in the nest; but the male drives them away harshly. This is part of the selection process; the male is looking for females who are very sexually motivated, and his aggressive manner frightens away the faint-hearted.

When a male is ready to take a female to his nest, he

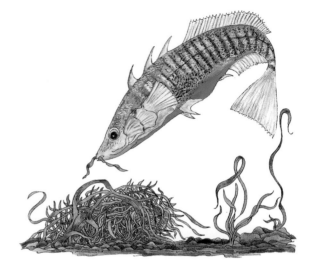

The male stickleback builds a nest in spring in readiness for mating.

courts the fish of his choice and they perform a zigzag dance. The dance sequence is a chain of interactions between the male and female, in which neither will proceed from one act to another unless suitable response actions are made. The male will not lead a female to his nest unless every step in the set routine has been carried out; then he entices her down. He points at the entrance with his head and chivvies the female fish into the tunnel. When she enters, the male butts her sides and trembles to stimulate her spawning; she lays her eggs, and he follows her to fertilize them by shedding milt (sperm) into the water around the eggs.

The female is driven away by the male, who then stays on guard, fanning the water with his tail to make sure the water is well supplied with oxygen. Occasionally a water snail may wander over the nest; if it is small, the male stickleback will carry it away. If the snail is large it poses a bit of a problem, but vigorous prodding causes it to withdraw into its shell, and then it is easily pushed away from the nest to the stickleback's satisfaction.

After a week or so, depending on the water temperature, the eggs hatch. The male prevents the fry from straying far; if any do wander off, he sucks them into his mouth and spits them back into the nest. The little sticklebacks are soon big enough to fend for themselves and they disperse.

Sticklebacks will breed in a cold water aquarium, where a regular addition of live water fleas (*Daphnia* species) and bloodworms will keep them well fed and healthy. Prepare a tank as suggested on page 78; establish a male in the tank first and, when he has started to build a nest, hold a mirror to the outside of the glass to see how he reacts to what he assumes to be another male in his territory.

When I have kept breeding three-spined sticklebacks I have been very careful to keep anyone wearing red away from the tank, as the poor male becomes frantic at the sight of a huge competitor in his territory!

Notice how quickly the breeding colours fade after serving their purpose of attracting the opposite sex and warning off rivals.

Put the sticklebacks back where you found them when the fry disperse.

The zigzag courtship dance is a series of interactions. The female arrives – the fish dance – the male courts – the male leads – the female follows – the male shows her the nest – the female enters and spawns – the male fertilizes the eggs and drives the female away.

Freshwater Wonders

*A sedge warbler and, on the right, a
reed warbler with its nest.*

I love to kneel by a pond and gaze into its mysterious depths, especially when the warmth of the spring sun spreads through the water, waking the animals from their winter quiescence amongst the plants or in the mud below. Life in the pond begins to take on a sense of urgency; frogs, toads, newts and fish begin courting, mating and laying eggs; water fleas and other minute animals and plants 'bloom', providing food for larger creatures; and other forms of life prepare to grow and reproduce, making the underwater world one of endless movement and surprise.

In summer there is a time of departure, when tiny frogs, toads and newts climb out of the water to hunt and grow on land. Mayflies, alder flies and caddis flies drag themselves free of the surface film to spend a short time on the wing, mating and dancing over the water that has been home to them for a year or more. Damselfly and dragonfly nymphs complete their miracle of metamorphosis, from underwater predator to scintillating aviator with sparkling livery and dazzling wings, matchless in their skills of hunting and flying. Frogs laze in the sun, diving into the water to swim effortlessly away at the merest hint of a footfall; newts bask just below the water surface, while pond skaters and water striders show the ease with which they 'walk on water'.

The richness and variety of animal life in a pond depend on the plants, for it is these which provide food, shelter and nesting sites for aquatic creatures. The many tadpoles, water snails and insect larvae who graze on the plants are preyed upon by beetles and their larvae, dragonfly nymphs, newts and small fish. These predators may, in their turn, be eaten by larger fish, frogs, visiting herons or mammals such as water shrews and mink.

With so many predators around, death is a constant threat, silently stalking the quiet deep; when death strikes, in come the cleaners – water slaters, midge larvae and water snails – preparing the bodies for their transformation into the raw materials for fresh plant growth.

Ponds have been a source of fascination for me for a long time, and at Bracken Hall I kept as many different pond creatures as I could. It gave me a wonderful opportunity to watch the complete life-cycles of animals which you often see, but never seem to understand fully. Day in and day out I watched the tapestry of life in freshwater unfolding, revealing secrets that filled me with wonder, and answering questions I hadn't even thought of asking.

LIFE IN FRESHWATER

Water exerts pressure in all directions. Many of the organisms living in water are very delicate, and the water which surrounds them gives them support. Submerged water plants are supported by the surrounding water; you can prove this by taking a plant out of the water. The plant that looked so beautiful underwater, floating gracefully upwards with its leaves expanded, crumples into a soggy mass as it is lifted out of the supporting medium. Put it back and it returns to its lovely form.

The pressure of water increases with depth; so the upward pressure is greater than the downward pressure, giving a lifting force within the water. This is called buoyancy. If you push the closed end of a tumbler beneath the surface of water in a bowl, you can feel the upward thrust of the water on the bottom of the tumbler. The gases inside water plants give the plants added buoyancy.

Many small water animals have to hold on to plants when they are at rest, or they would be carried upwards to the water surface. For example, leeches have suckers and most water insects have a claw at the tip of each foot with which they are able to grip. Other animals are able to remain suspended in the water; if you have a water

Here is the life cycle of a common frog, showing the four month development and metamorphosis from egg to tiny froglet. After leaving the pond, three or four years pass before the frog is sexually mature.

butt you will probably find a phantom midge larva in there. This is the transparent, carnivorous larva of a biting midge, which normally lies motionless, suspended horizontally in water. Put a phantom midge larva in a jar of water; the only easily visible structures in the clear body are the black eyes and the two pairs of air-filled sacs which help the larva keep its equilibrium in water. Fish have a gas-filled swim-bladder whose volume can be adjusted to the depth the fish wishes to swim in, so the animal is kept buoyant.

Water has a high surface tension; the liquid surface is an incredibly thin membrane in a state of tension, like a tightly stretched elastic skin. It also has considerable strength, as it is able to support anything whose weight is insufficient to break its continuity.

Look at the surface of water in a glass. The curving of the surface is called the meniscus; the surface film is pulled down at the centre by gravity. Test the surface tension by filling a small bowl with water and placing a piece of blotting paper on the water surface. Put a needle on to the blotting paper. The paper will soak up water and sink, leaving the needle floating on the water surface. Using paper keeps the surface film intact; try floating the needle without using paper. Carefully add a little washing up liquid and see what happens.

Some small animals are able to walk on water; these include springtails, water striders and pond skaters. Watch a pond skater on the surface of a pond; its weight causes little saucer-like depressions in the surface film. Most insects have little claws on the tips of their feet; these would pierce the surface film and the animal would fall through. Insects that walk on water have a fan of water-resistant hairs at the tips of their feet.

Have you ever fallen into a swimming pool? The water resistance slaps very hard at solid bodies – however small. It is very important to remember that point when returning animals to their watery habitats. Gently lower the container with the animals into the water, and allow the animals to move out of the container under the water at their own pace.

Living in moving water must be like constantly battling against a gale force wind – a tug of war with the current. Many animals are adapted to life in moving water with its high oxygen content, and they manage to resist the current in several ways.

A logical way of staying put is to use an anchor, and a number of animals use suckers for this purpose.

The blackfly larva has two suckers, one at the base of the body and the other at the base of the fleshy proleg behind the head. The larva usually only has the basal

The springtail has a forked tail which is held by a sucker-like appendage under the body. When the tail is released it hits the water with such a force that the animal is propelled into the air.
Springtails are found in groups at the edge of still water.

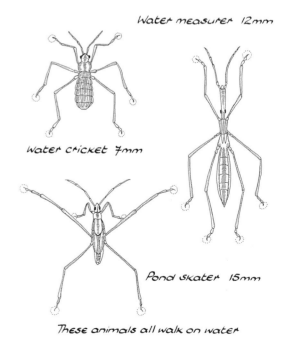

Water measurer 12mm

Water cricket 7mm

Pond skater 15mm

These animals all walk on water

sucker in action, but in a very fast current the anterior sucker is also used.

Some species of mayfly nymphs are adapted to the conditions in moving water. The nymph of *Rhithrogena semicolorata*, known as the olive upright, has its first pair of gills modified to form a simple sucker beneath its body, enabling it to cling to stones. Other clinging mayfly nymphs are shaped like teardrops; the broad, flattened head faces the current and the body is tapered. As water flows over such a shape it forces it down, not along.

Caddis-fly larvae living in swiftly flowing streams tend to make their cases of stones, and they are able to anchor the cases down with silken threads.

Flatworms secrete a slime track into which thousands of fine hair-like structures called cilia beat in a wave-like action. These miniature anchors allow the flatworm to glide over the stones on the stream bed, working like a velcro fastening.

Some animals prefer to burrow or hide to avoid being swept away by the current. Nymphs of the mayfly *Ephemera danica* have shovel-like forelegs and upper jaws shaped like tusks, enabling them to dig burrows in fine sand and silt.

The miller's thumb, or bull head, is a fish designed in a teardrop shape for life in swift-flowing water; it is camouflaged so as to be almost invisible as it waits near the stony stream bed for unsuspecting prey.

Plants adapt themselves to different situations, too; some plants produce variously shaped leaves to suit their surroundings. Water crowfoot, for instance, has lobed leaves which float on the water surface, while the finely divided submerged leaves offer a low resistance to water movement.

If you look at the vegetation in and around a freshwater pond or river, you may see several distinct communities of plants, each more or less confined to a particular area. Freshwater habitats are divided into zones; the zones are not completely separate, as some species of plants and animals overlap the life zones. There are totally submerged plants rooted in mud. Some plants, such as duckweed and frogbit, float freely over the water surface with no roots attaching them to the bottom. Others, including broad-leaved pondweed and amphibious bistort, grow in shallower water and are rooted in mud, while at the water's edge water-cress, water plantain and many others grow in swampy conditions. In the surrounding moist ground, marsh plants such as marsh marigolds, bur-reed and reedmace grow in lush profusion, binding the mud with their roots and giving shelter to birds and small mammals.

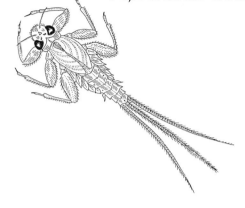

The nymph of the mayfly RHITHROGENA SEMICOLORATA is 13mm long & is adapted to life in fast-flowing water. The nymph's body is flattened in shape to withstand the current.

The chart overleaf shows a selection of fresh water plants, many of which carry the eggs of aquatic animals.

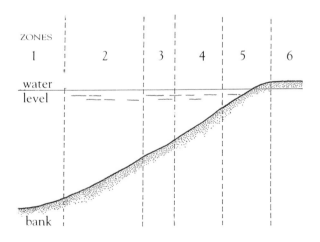

Here is a zone profile across a pond to show the zonation of plants.
Zones 1 and 2 are water meadows of totally submerged plants.
Zone 3 is an area of floating plants.
Zone 4 has rooted plants with floating leaves.
Zone 5 has swamp plants and Zone 6 has marsh plants.

65

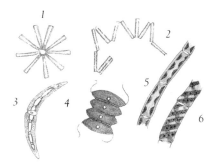

Phytoplankton – microscopic plants which float freely in water. 1 and 2 are diatoms; 3 is a desmid; 4 and 6 are green algae and 5 is a yellow-green alga.

Spiked water-milfoil, a submerged plant of still and running water. The flower spike emerges in mid summer. The silver beetle's silky egg case contains 50-60 eggs; the hollow mast provides them with air.

Water violet, a submerged plant of shallow, slow-moving water. The flower spike emerges in late spring or early summer. The eggs are those of the lesser water boatman.

Fennel-leaved pond weed is a submerged plant of still and running water. The flower spike emerges in summer. The green hydra could easily be overlooked.

Grassy pondweed is a submerged plant which grows to 1 metre (over 3 ft) long in still waters. The female water spider has put many eggs into the safety of her diving bell.

Perfoliate pondweed is a submerged plant of still and running water. The flower spike emerges in mid to late summer. The eggs in a ring of jelly are those of a caddis fly.

Duckweeds are floating plants of still water. 1 is great duckweed; 2 is gibbous duckweed; 3 is ivy-leaved duckweed and 4 is the floating egg of a mosquito, Anopheles species.

Frogbit is a floating plant of still and slow-moving water, flowering in summer. The jelly sac contains the eggs of a non-biting midge, Chironomus plumosus.

Amphibious bistort, a floating-leaved plant of still and slow-moving waters, flowering early summer to early autumn. The red eggs are those of a water mite.

Watercress forms masses at the edge of clean water; it flowers from late spring to mid-autumn. The brown egg capsule is that of a leech.

Arrowhead is an emergent plant which often grows in mud, flowering early to mid-summer. Alderfly eggs are laid in batches on leaves overhanging the water.

Water plantain is an emergent plant whose roots bind mud. The eggs are those of a common frog.

Water starwort is a submerged plant of still and running water. The larva and pupa are those of the buffalo midge, found in running water.

Hornwort is a submerged plant of still and slow-moving water. The egg raft belongs to the mosquito Culex species.

Canadian pondweed is a submerged plant of still and slow-moving waters. The eggs are those of a newt, who lays her eggs singly, wrapping each one in a leaf.

Curly pondweed is a submerged plant of still and running water. The flower spike emerges from early summer to early autumn. The jelly-covered eggs are those of a great pond snail.

Willow moss forms underwater meadows which give shelter to many animals. The eggs and larva are those of a pike.

Stonewort is another deep-water plant, affording good shelter and spawning grounds. The shy kingfisher perches above the water, watching for prey.

Broad-leaved pondweed is a floating-leaved plant of still water, flowering in summer. The eggs are those of a great diving beetle.

The yellow water-lily is a floating-leaved plant of still waters, flowering in summer. The larva is that of the china mark moth above.

Water crowfoot has lobed, floating leaves and finely divided submerged leaves; it flowers in summer. The egg strings are those of a common toad.

Bur-reed forms clumps on marshy ground. Water voles live in waterside burrows, harmlessly eating the plants on the water's edge.

Great reedmace grows to 2 metres (6 ft 6 in) on marshy ground. The sedge warbler hunts for insects in the reed beds.

The common reed grows to 4 metres (13 ft) on marshy ground. The reed warbler weaves a neat cup-shaped nest around reed stems.

REPRODUCTION

The death and subsequent decay of plants can completely alter a stretch of water. Marginal plants fall and form a mat of vegetation in which silt and humus can accumulate; this causes the water to become shallower, and reed beds are succeeded by marshland. Trees which favour marshy ground begin to colonize, forming alder or willow carr. This is the process called plant succession (see page 27). You have probably seen how quickly a neglected garden goes 'wild' or a disused railway becomes overgrown. No area remains static, as the processes of plant succession are always at work.

The plant life of freshwater habitats is very important to the animals who depend upon the water. Plants provide oxygen and food; their leaves and stems provide support, shelter from predators and shade from the sun. Plants provide sites on which to deposit eggs and, in some cases, in which the eggs can develop.

Many of the eggs you may find on plants in and around a pond are encased in protective jelly. This is certainly true of frog spawn; the jelly protection means that the spawn can stand being frozen for up to twelve hours without the developing tadpoles being harmed. In the case of toads, the strings of jelly-covered eggs are wrapped around the stems of water plants in the warmer levels of water. The jelly is a deterrent to would-be predators, but it is often the first food of the hatching young who eat themselves free.

Some dragonflies and water beetles put their eggs into plant tissue; flatworms, leeches and oligochaete worms lay their eggs *en masse* in a cocoon, which is then deposited on stones or on to plants.

Many eggs are simply put into the water at random to take their chance in the not-too-friendly depths, but some parents do care for their eggs. Male three-spined sticklebacks (see page 60) are good fathers, protecting their young in a nest until the tiny fish are a few weeks old. Freshwater shrimps are often seen in pairs; the larger male swims with the female until the eggs are fertilized. The female carries her eggs in a brood pouch between her leg bases, and here the eggs develop into tiny replicas of the adult. Male and female water lice (*Asellus* species) also swim in tandem until the eggs are laid into a brood pouch, where the young remain for a few days after hatching.

The female swan mussel lays up to a million tiny eggs, which she carries in a brood pouch in her gill region for several months. During this time they develop into a larval form, and are then dispersed into the water.

Water scorpions feign dead when caught. They are carnivores. Eggs are laid individually on plants just below the water surface. The nymphs are smaller than the adults with a very short breathing tube & no wings. Development to the adult stage is gradual.

The swan mussel is a freshwater bi-valve mollusc. The glochidium larva is cast out to become a parasite on fish until it grows bigger.

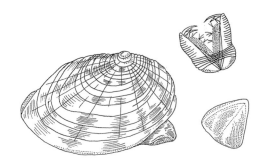

The larvae, called glochidia, are eaten by many predators; but some become attached to fish upon whom they feed parasitically, until the growing larvae change into young mussels.

The larvae of water mites behave parasitically, often attaching themselves to aquatic insects. You may find insects with red mites on them, both in and out of water. I once found a dor beetle that was completely infested by red mites; harvestmen often have one or two mites hanging on to them and late summer bumble bees may be pestered by mites.

Female water fleas carry eggs inside a brood pouch. These eggs are unfertilized – parthenogenic – and they are all female. Male water fleas are only produced in unfavourable conditions and the fertilized eggs, laid after mating has taken place, develop tough shells able to resist drought and freezing conditions.

A hydra can reproduce asexually by budding. A tiny new hydra develops on the body of the parent; the base then separates & the little hydra breaks free.

RUTHLESS KILLERS
Great Diving Beetles

Great diving beetles are amazing; they are capable of flying from pond to pond, and yet they are totally at home under water. They are very rewarding creatures to watch and they can easily be kept in a covered aquarium where they may live for two or three years.

The beetle's oval body is dark green above and bright yellow below, with a yellow body trim and legs. The male has smooth elytra (wing cases) and sucker pads on his front legs, while the female has grooved elytra and no sucker pads. The eyes are large and bright, situated at the sides of the head so that the beetle can see above and below its body. Each eye has about 9,000 tiny units called facets and the beetles miss very little; they are fierce and greedy predators.

The hind legs are highly adapted, being fringed with long, stiff hairs which spread out during the 'pull' stroke and flatten during the return stroke, so 'feathering' the rowing legs and enabling the beetles to swim strongly.

Breathing takes place at the water surface where the beetle sticks out its back end, raises the elytra slightly and takes in air through large spiracles or air vents. When the beetle returns under water, it appears to have a silvery end to its body. This air bubble is slowly used up; the time taken to use the air varies according to the beetle's activities and the temperature of the water. The warmer the water, the less oxygen there is in it and the more rapidly diffusion will take place.

Great diving beetles fly in the air and swim in the water. Male great diving beetles have suction pads on their front legs. The larvae are fierce predators.

It is better not to handle water beetles; use a net or jar when it is necessary to move them. Great diving beetles may try to nip your finger and they have a pair of sharp spikes on their underside. Another defence mechanism is their ability to produce an unpleasant-smelling nerve poison from glands on the thorax; this is lethal enough to kill a frog.

It is advisable to keep only one male beetle with two or three females. The females are very productive and lay white cigar-shaped eggs about 6 mm (¼ in) long, inserting them into the stems of water plants. The larvae that emerge from the eggs are even more aggressive than their parents; so fierce in fact that they have earned the name 'water tigers'.

Each larva is elongated, segmented and slightly flattened, with three pairs of legs that act as oars and a pair of tail-like appendages which are raised above the water surface when air is being taken in through the spiracles.

The larva will eat anything it can catch, including its own kind. Digestive juices are pumped into the victim from the larva's curved mandibles; the resulting fluid is drawn out, leaving only an empty skin. The larva is fully grown in six to eight weeks, and at this stage it must be able to leave the water and find damp soil in which to burrow, or it will drown. The larva twists round and round in the soil to make a hollow in which it pupates, and a few weeks later the adult beetle emerges.

It is characteristic of some insect larvae to emerge from the egg looking very different to the adults; but there are some who closely resemble the parent except in size and the lack of wings and sexual organs. These young insects are called nymphs. Examples of this form of growth are found in the development of dragonflies, damselflies, stoneflies, mayflies, grasshoppers, earwigs and aphids.

As the nymph wanders about in its particular habitat, it feeds and grows until it becomes too big for its skin; the skin of an insect is a hard external skeleton unable to expand. So the exoskeleton has to split and allow the nymph to climb out of its restricting grip; each time this happens the nymph emerges looking more adult, with wing buds that are a little larger. As with caterpillars, the stage between each moult is called an instar. Moulting can take place many times during the development of some insects, though between four and ten is usual.

When we kept great diving beetles at our countryside centre, we were surprised at the way the beetles sometimes co-operated when catching food. Two or three of them would surround a large pond snail and winkle it out from its shell before devouring it.

From top to bottom. *Great diving beetle larva taking in air; the adult male chasing a tadpole while the female leaves her eggs inside the stem of an aquatic plant. Another larva sucks the juice of a tadpole.*

EPHEMERAL MAYFLIES

Mayflies are not confined to the month of May, despite their common name. Nor are they true flies, as mayflies usually have four wings and true flies only two.

Adult mayflies have reduced mouth parts and do not feed; so, as you can imagine, they do not live very long. Their short life is reflected in the name of the order – Ephemeroptera – from the Greek *ephemeros*, meaning living for a day.

There are about 200 species of mayfly in Britain and Europe; most are small insects with two or three long 'tails'. Fishermen are familiar with many mayfly species, as the insects are the models for the artificial flies used by anglers.

The nymphs of mayflies take a variety of forms according to their habitat. There are nymphs with flattened bodies, adapted to clinging to stones in fast-moving water; nymphs with streamlined bodies who swim actively; cylindrical nymphs with shovel-shaped forelegs for burrowing in sand and silt; and others which crawl about the low-growing vegetation of still waters.

Mayflies are easy to keep in an aquarium free of predators. They feed mainly on algae, which they scrape from stones and from soft plant material. One species, *Cloeon dipterum*, is good to watch, as the nymphs are agile and climb about among the water plants.

Mayfly nymphs have three long tail filaments, though at the final moult of some species (including *C. dipterum* the middle 'tail' disappears and the adult emerges with only two tails. All the nymphs have gills on the segments of their abdomen, enabling oxygen to be absorbed from the water. Most nymphs take about a year to develop, or a little longer, and they may moult many times.

Mayflies are unique among insects in moulting after they become winged. The well-formed nymph in its final instar floats to the water surface, where the nymphal skin splits and a dull winged insect climbs out. This is the sub-imago. Its wings are covered with very fine hairs and are not very strong, so the mayfly 'dun' is governed by air currents at this stage. The sub-imagos that reach a suitable resting place moult again and the shiny winged 'spinners' emerge to dance over the water surface.

It is usually the male mayflies who dance over the water while they await the arrival of females. Watch the dancing mayflies on a warm, still day, the graceful aerial flutterings of the whole crowd, gently rising and falling. Occasionally a pair will leave quietly, not disturbing the slow rhythm of the dance. They mate on the wing, and the eggs are laid into the water.

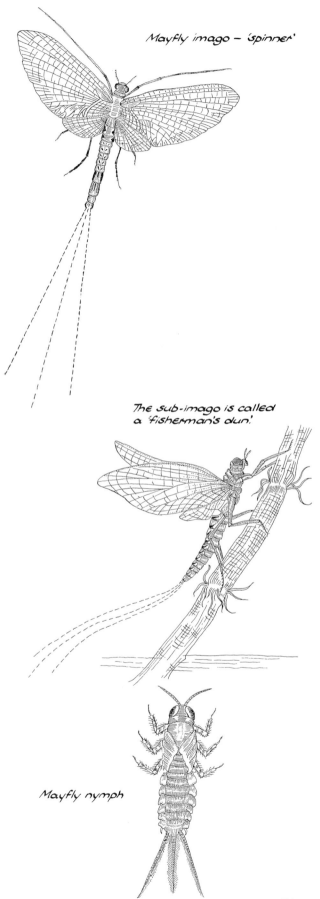

Mayfly imago – 'spinner'

The sub-imago is called a 'fisherman's dun.'

Mayfly nymph

DRAGONS AND DAMSELS

Dragonflies, not unlike those we see today, were flying in the swampy forests of Britain 250 million years ago. They are the earliest known winged insects, and fossil records show some very large ones, with a wing span of 70 cm (27 in). Dragonflies and damselflies both belong to the order Odonata; but after five minutes at the side of a pond watching the insects in action you will see the difference between the two groups.

Dragonflies are usually large, stout-bodied insects with a strong flight; their hind wings have a broader base than their forewings and, because the muscles have only a simple up and down pivot action, the wings are held horizontally even when the insect is at rest.

When seen from above, the dragonfly's large eyes appear to be meeting on top of the head, whereas those of the damselfly are set well apart. Damselflies are dainty in build with slender bodies and a darting flight. The damselflies' four wings are all similar in shape; when at rest they are held close together over the back.

Dragonflies and damselflies are highly specialized in the craft of hunting and capturing other insects on the wing. With their large efficient eyes, they are able to spot prey 12 metres (40 ft) away in almost any direction. Dragonfly eyes are highly developed; each eye takes up the whole of one side of the head and is composed of up to 28,000 facets, each of them like a miniature telescope. The legs are arranged so that, when they are spread, they form a basket which helps to scoop up flying insects; however, this leg arrangement makes walking a very awkward activity.

Dragonflies and damselflies share a unique mating procedure. The male insect transfers sperm from the end of his abdomen to special pairing organs on the second segment of his abdomen, near to his thorax. The male holds the back of the female's head with his tail claspers, and the female curves her abdomen underneath the male. Her genital opening now comes into contact with the special apparatus at the front of the male's abdomen, and the sperm is transferred to the female.

All this takes place in flight, and the insects are said to be flying in tandem. In some species, the pair stay in tandem until egg-laying has taken place, the male holding on to a plant close to the water surface, while the female enters the water, either wholly or partly, and deposits her eggs on submerged objects or into slits made in water plants. This summer we watched a golden-ringed dragonfly, *Cordulegaster boltonii*, put eggs into one of the ponds. It took about an hour and a half of

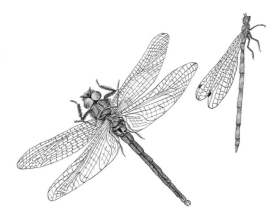

Dragonflies have fixed wings; damselflies fold theirs when at rest.

Dragonfly nymph

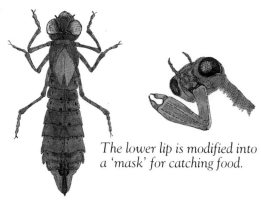

The lower lip is modified into a 'mask' for catching food.

Damselfly nymph

concentrated work, and the lone female went to a lot of trouble in her efforts not to put eggs in the same place twice.

Two or three dragonfly nymphs will live together in a tank so long as they are well fed on bloodworms, water fleas or tadpoles. They are fierce carnivores and can become cannibalistic. Below the mouth, the nymph has an extendible, elongated and hinged 'mask', which varies in shape according to the species. The dark green or brown nymph merges into the background of the habitat and waits for an unsuspecting victim to draw near. Then the mask shoots forward and the prey is caught in the claws of the mask, which is retracted to bring the victim close to the captor's jaws.

I find the large hawker dragonfly nymphs the most rewarding to watch, my favourite being the emperor dragonflies. The nymphs moult between ten and fifteen times during their two to five years under water; each time a skin is shed, the nymph is a step nearer to becoming an adult.

When watching animals closely all day and every day, you notice when they don't eat and wonder why. When a fat dragonfly nymph goes off its food, it is very likely time for it to shed its skin. This is a very vulnerable time for any insect because, when the hard old exoskeleton is shed, it takes some hours for the new, soft skin to harden and darken in colour. I love to watch the brown dragonfly nymph skin crack down the back of the thorax as the nymph inflates itself. Out of this old skin steps a larger, green nymph, delicately drawing each new leg out of the old brown 'stockings'. It is a wonderful thing to see; but the final moult, the emergence of the adult insect is an extravaganza!

When you set up a tank for dragonfly nymphs, push some strong twigs into the gravel, to rise above the water surface, so that the nymphs can climb out of the water when they are ready to become adults.

The changing of one skin for another is dangerous, but climbing out of a nymphal skin as a flying insect is far more so; and because of the dangers it usually takes place at night. By watching the nymphs daily, and seeing how they are behaving, you can get a fair idea of when the dragonfly is likely to emerge. Watch just before midsummer for one of the larger dragonfly nymphs becoming sluggish, not eating and spending long periods of time clasping one of the twigs that stick out of the water. I have watched this preparation time so often and it still makes my heart leap with excitement, because this is the whole point of existence for that particular dragonfly; the time of rebirth as an ethereal being.

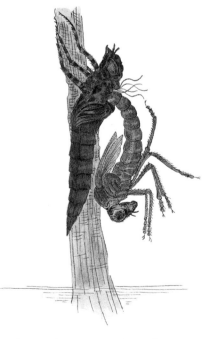

A dragonfly emerging from the nymphal skin.

Gradually the exoskeleton loosens and the green and blue of the adult dragonfly can be seen faintly through the thin brown outer covering. The nymph changes its breathing mechanism – from breathing under water to breathing free air – while at the same time the format of the mouth parts changes.

The nymph slowly drags itself further up the twig, then the thorax splits neatly, exposing the dragonfly colours inside the nymphal skin. Slowly, so slowly, the dragonfly head is pushed through this opening, which seems far too small. This part of the metamorphosis always reminds me of a human baby being born and I find it very moving.

When the head and thorax of the dragonfly have emerged from the brown nymph shell, the insect rests with its head hanging back and down. This period of suspension lasts for about three quarters of an hour, and a pool of excess water drips from the dragonfly. At last, the head and thorax jerk up and the dragonfly creeps forward, drawing its wings, abdomen and legs out of the nymphal shell.

The wings are crumpled and small at first, but very slowly they begin to expand, the wrinkles ironing themselves out. Now is the time to look at the beauty of the dragonfly; to marvel at the wonderful eyes, so large that they meet at the top of the head. Look closely at the facets of the compound eyes; no wonder the dragonfly is such a great hunter, with vision such as this at its command. Notice the short antennae and the strong biting mouth parts; look at the slender neck which enables the head to swivel, giving all-round vision.

The slim abdomen is segmented and very beautiful in colour. The colours are produced by structural effects which catch the light or by pigments, so after death the colours disappear. By this time the wings have expanded and you can see that the forewings are a slightly different shape to the hind wings. The dragonfly will cling to the twig in the tank until it is thoroughly dry. After I have looked my fill, I carry the twig carefully into the garden and stick it firmly into the earth, so that the dragonfly can leave when it is ready.

Most dragonflies live for about a month or six weeks. They are often found a long way from water, feeding well on other flying insects.

Some people are afraid of dragonflies because they are such large insects. They imagine that they can sting, but I can assure you that dragonflies do not have stings and are quite harmless. Their country names of 'devil's darning needle' and 'sewing needle', do little to improve their reputation!

A common frog, its eggs and water plantain

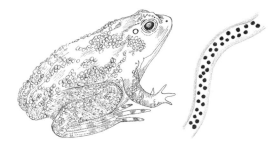

This is a rough-skinned, common toad with a ribbon of eggs.

While the mouth is forming, the tadpole is nourished by the remains of the yolk sac in its stomach. When the mouth has formed, the tadpole begins to eat algae and soft leaf tissue, breathing by means of three external gills. Watch these gills, for they soon become covered by a flap of skin. The tadpole then breathes through a spiracle, an air vent, in the left hand side; this is connected to an internal gill cavity.

Usually, hind leg stumps appear after five weeks. If the legs are very late in appearing, you could add a few drops of iodine to the water of one of your containers. Iodine is necessary for the production of the hormones which control the change from tadpole to frog or toad. Two weeks after the legs appear, the toes develop on the feet.

The tadpoles soon stop being plant eaters, and will need meat to eat. Live daphnia and bloodworms kept in the tank will overcome any tendency to cannibalism at this stage; alternatives to live food may be small pinches of 'ants' eggs' or a piece of raw meat dangled in the water for short periods. I always feed tadpoles on live food, as the 'food' helps to keep the water clean while it is waiting to be eaten.

At about eight weeks, the lungs develop and the tadpoles begin to gulp air. The front legs begin to grow by about week ten, and the tail is slowly absorbed.

Put the froglets into a suitable habitat when they begin to come out of the water. It is usually better to put them back near the pond where they were spawned if this is possible; don't forget to wet your hand before you lift them out of the tank.

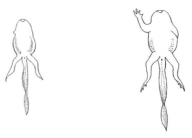

The hind legs grow first, followed by the left foreleg & then the right foreleg.

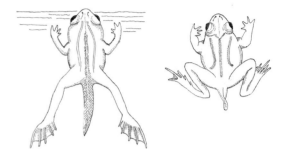

The tail shortens as it is internally digested & absorbed; soon the froglet will be ready to leave the water. It takes three or four years for frogs & toads to develop sexually, & many die before then.

THE GENTEEL COURTSHIP OF NEWTS

Unlike female frogs and toads, a female newt is able to choose her partner and may court and mate with more than one male.

Newts are rather unusual, because although fertilization takes place internally, the males of most species do not copulate with the females; instead, sperm is deposited on the bottom of the habitat in a capsule called a spermatophore. This is taken up by the female into her cloaca, or genital opening, where the sperm swim to the eggs and fertilize them before they are laid.

Newts are very secretive and their slow, careful courtship is not at all like the loud, rough frolics of the frogs and toads.

Male newts are very colourful in spring. Male palmate newts develop webs between the digits of their back feet;

male smooth newts grow an undulating crest from the back of the head to the end of the tail and under the tail; the large male great crested newt produces a spiky crest on his back, with an interruption at the base of the tail, but continuing along both top and bottom edges.

Courtship proceedings begin when the male and female meet by chance; the ritual varies according to the species, but the basic principles are similar. The male sniffs at the female's cloaca, probably to assess her breeding condition; she usually swims away, establishing a passive role. The male tries to take up a position in front of the female, raising his crest and fanning his tail backwards and forwards along his body, so that the water currents carry his smell towards the female.

Soon a sense of urgency creeps in, and the male begins to nudge and head-butt the female's sides. When she is ready, she will respond by moving towards the male; but he retreats, still displaying. If the female continues to follow, he turns and crawls away from her; the female follows and touches his tail with her snout. This is the signal for the male to deposit a spermatophore; he creeps away from it, then stops with his tail folded against the side of his body. He has moved only far enough to ensure that, when the female moves forward to touch his tail again, she will stop with her cloaca above the spermatophore. She stops as planned, and the sperm packet is drawn into the female's body. This sequence may be repeated two or three times, increasing the chance of fertilization, but many sequences are aborted.

Within a few days the female begins to lay about 300 jelly-covered eggs; each one is deposited in a folded leaf to protect it from predators. As you may imagine, it takes the female many long hours to lay each egg so carefully.

Newt tadpoles dart about. They have feathery gills which are retained until they are almost ready to leave the water, when they are absorbed. The tiny front legs develop a week or so after hatching, and are soon followed by the hind legs.

AQUARIUM CARE
Keep them Healthy and Happy

Watching small animals in habitats of your own creation is fun. One particular lesson to be learned is that the animals you keep are totally at your mercy, dependent on you for food, health and comfort.

Many of the points that follow may seem off-putting, but they are not meant to be. You will learn by

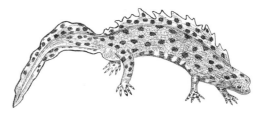

A male great crested newt in courtship splendour

A female great crested newt stands with her cloaca over a spermatophore at the end of a courtship dance.

Newt tadpoles usually take about three months to metamorphose; they become sexually mature in their third or fourth year.

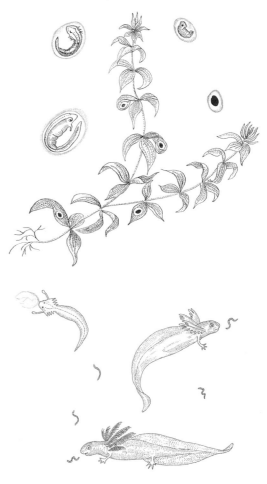

experience; but it is sad to lose the contents of an aquarium and maybe my experience will help you to avoid a disaster.

It is important to keep everything very clean, including your hands. Set up freshwater tanks (aquaria) about a week before introducing any animals, so that plants can become established. It isn't necessary to have a pump for aeration unless the animals are adapted for life in fast moving water.

A glass-sided tank is ideal; it must be thoroughly cleaned and rinsed. Gravel makes the best base for the habitat; builder's sand or soil is unsuitable, as it becomes stale very quickly and the water doesn't clear. Wash the gravel under a running tap until the water runs clear.

Slope the gravel from the back of the tank towards the front, so there is at least 25 mm (1 in) at the front and twice this depth at the back. This ensures that debris will mostly collect at the front. It can then be removed using a siphon, though siphons have a nasty habit of sucking up little animals! I prefer to see water lice and bloodworms cleaning up a well-balanced tank.

Use well-scrubbed and scalded rocks or large stones from a garden to create a background with plenty of hiding places. It isn't advisable to use stones from the seaside, as they often contain minerals detrimental to freshwater life.

Wash water plants well and remove any dead leaves. Take away some of the jelly-covered batches of snail eggs which may be clinging to the plant. A few snails are useful, but if you have too many they will quickly eat up the vegetation.

Push the base of the plant stems sideways into the gravel and anchor them with a large stone. Plants produce oxygen in daylight, but use oxygen and produce carbon dioxide in darkness. Too many plants will make it difficult for the animals to breathe at night.

Before filling the tank, make sure that it isn't standing in full sunlight. The sun will warm the water and kill the animals; it certainly encourages algae to grow.

Using a jug or jar, pour the water *gently* on to one of the rocks so that the gravel and the plants remain undisturbed.

When you introduce animals to your tank, try to ensure that the temperature of the water they are entering is similar to that which they are leaving. Lower the animals into the water gently; don't let them fall in.

Tapping on the sides of the tank sends shock waves through the water and hurts the animals. **Don't do it.**

Many aquarium shops sell live daphnia and bloodworms; or you may know a pond or a water butt

Water vole among bur-reed

where you can collect midge larvae. These are ideal for feeding fish, carnivorous insects and tadpoles.

Before you put other animals into an established tank, be sure that it isn't going to be overcrowded; and that you aren't putting predators in with prey or vice versa. From this point of view, it is as well to keep great diving beetles and dragonfly nymphs in tanks of their own, with only food and snails as company.

Keep only two or three great diving beetle larvae in a small tank. When they are well grown, slope the tank sideways by firmly wedging it under one end. At the shallow end, simulate a bank; sphagnum moss is a clean material to use for this purpose. When the larvae are ready to pupate, they must be able to leave the water or they will drown.

Tanks containing great diving beetles or water spiders will need tops. These may be of glass or plastic, resting on pieces of wood to allow air to get in, but I would recommend fine gauze or very fine net curtaining which can be tied over the top of the aquarium.

Dust will settle on the surface of the water in an uncovered tank; this can be scooped off with a jar and carefully replaced with fresh water. In warm weather, the water in the tanks will quickly become stale: ladle out about half the water and replace it gently with water that has been standing in a cool place. Remember to let tap water stand overnight before using it in a tank.

It is not a good idea to keep frogs, toads or newts for more than two or three days. Frogs and toads eat moving food, such as flies; this sort of food is difficult to supply constantly. Amphibians don't really like living in a vivarium and they act as though they are in prison.

Newts need specialist care. They can climb out of a tank that has the slightest gap in the lid. For a special treat, keep a pair of common newts for a few days in spring to watch their courtship; but then put them back where you found them very carefully.

The Wildlife and Countryside Act of 1981 protects many plants and animals including frogs, toads and newts. It is illegal to kill, injure, capture or sell these protected animals without a licence. It is also illegal to damage or destroy any place which these animals use as a shelter, or to disturb them while they are there. Great crested newts and natterjack toads are specially protected. This means that you may not even *handle* them without a licence.

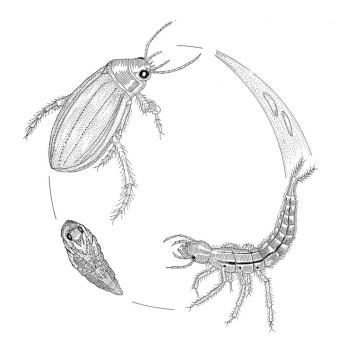

Female great diving beetles lay eggs into plant tissue. The carnivorous larva rises to the water surface to take in air. The larva pupates out of water in damp soil or mud. Great diving beetles can fly as well as they can swim.

ALTERNATIVES TO TANKS

It may be that keeping an aquarium is out of the question for you. If so, try raising small insects in large jars or bowls. Midge larvae may not sound very exciting but their life-cycles are interesting. One or two caddis worms can be kept in a large jar, and mayfly nymphs don't need a great deal of space.

Water snails can be raised from eggs and the adult behaviour observed in a small container. As the snail moves slowly along the glass, watch the bands of muscle across the foot. Does their position remain the same? What is their function? See how the snail eats algae from the glass by rasping with its tongue or radula. The radula is a continually growing strip bearing rows of horny teeth; when they wear out, the snail swallows them and the next set move forward. When the snails have mated, how long is it before the eggs are laid, and how long does it take the eggs to hatch? How does the snail breathe? How often does it fill its lung? Mark the snails' shells carefully with animal marking paint, so that you can keep records and compare their behaviour.

Everything in nature is interesting to observe, however small it may be, particularly when you have learned to ask the right questions. Keep the animal numbers low, and you will be able to watch plenty of action in miniature.

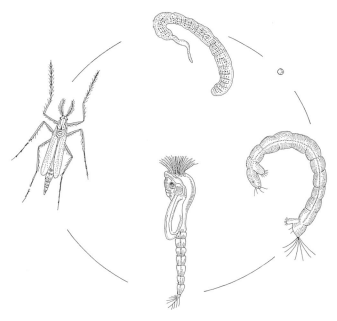

The eggs of non-biting midges are laid on to plants, just below the water surface. The detritus-eating larvae are the 'bloodworms' often found in water butts. The pupa cases resemble those of mosquitoes; the tuft of filaments absorbs dissolved oxygen from the water.

Life in a Field

There are some very old fields, surrounded by hedges or walls, that have their own names. Some of the names relate to people, some to old village matters, some to battles and some simply to their size or use. The field in which I am making my wild garden is called Barleyland; the one next to it is called Emma Croft.

Fields are fascinating things. Whether you think of a field as somewhere to play football or a hay meadow in summer, remember that underneath the turf or crops there is an underground world at work, and that among the grasses, animals play out their short lives. A field isn't just a field; it is a web of life.

GRASSES

Grasses are very important plants; wheat, oats, maize and barley are among the food crops in the grass family, and grass is the main food of most grazing animals.

When a grass seed germinates, it produces only one seed leaf or cotyledon. This puts grass into a plant group called monocotyledons (one seed leaf), separate from that of many other flowering plants which have two seed leaves and so belong to a group called dicotyledons. The leaves of monocotyledons are long and narrow with parallel veins; they are arranged in two alternate rows on round, hollow stems. Each leaf is made up of two parts: the blade – that is the broadest part that is free — and the sheath – the tubular or overlapping part that enfolds the grass stem.

Grass has a special way of growing that means it can be continually eaten and cut without the plant itself being destroyed. Grass buds are produced very close to the soil surface, so they are rarely damaged by grazing animals or mower blades. There is a growing point at the base of each leaf blade which constantly produces new cells so that, when the upper part of the leaf blade has been eaten or mown, new tissue is formed at the base.

The word field owes its origin to the Old English 'feld' – an area felled from the forest. The process of plant succession is always at work, and so the vegetation of a field is unstable. If grazing or hay-making stops, then shrubs have the opportunity to become established and the succession towards woodland begins. Crops must be sown and tended every year, or herbaceous plants will seed themselves down and become established.

Where grassland is not intensively grazed or managed for hay, there is a great deal of vegetative litter left at the end of the growing season. This layer of dead plant material is attacked by micro-organisms and by various animals which help in the decomposition process. Some of the leaf litter is eaten, but only a small portion is digested, much more being excreted without undergoing much change. The excreted parts are not wasted, as they are eaten by nemotodes, beetles and other soil invertebrates including many larvae. Their excreta in turn serve as food for others; and, so long as any energy-giving material remains, some organism will feed on it. The litter that isn't eaten breaks up into small pieces which, like the excreted matter, are decomposed by bacteria, fungi, earthworms and burying beetles.

There are many springtails (*Collembola* species) and mites (*Acari* species) amongst grassland litter; these feed

Opposite *is a picture of just a few of the plants and animals to be found in a hay meadow. A meadow is a field in which grasses and other plants grow up during the early summer, and are then cut to make hay. In this way, many spring-flowering plants are able to set their seeds before cutting begins, and some late-flowering herbaceous plants manage to survive too.*

Unfortunately, this ancient method of managing meadowland has, in all but a comparatively few cases, been taken over by modern farming methods. Many meadows have been drained and are regularly dressed with inorganic fertilizers. An application of nitrogen in late winter produces grass which can be grazed in spring; another application of inorganic fertilizer produces a hay crop in summer. These methods, plus the ploughing and reseeding with agriculturally improved grasses, have led to a serious threat to traditional hay meadows and rich, grazed pastures, thereby destroying the food supplies of many animals.

There are 43 plant and animal species in this picture. Try to find the seventeen plants: nettle, great burnet, meadow buttercup, pepper saxifrage, field poppy, harebell, cuckoo flower, St John's wort, meadow crane's bill, yellow rattle, ox-eye daisy, meadow saxifrage, white clover, dandelion, meadow fescue, meadow brome and timothy grass.

There are five mammals: hare, harvest mouse, rabbit, mole and field vole. The 21 invertebrates are: two-spot ladybird; red and black frog hopper bug; leaf beetle – Chaetocnema hortensis; leaf beetle – Chrysolina polita; violet ground beetle; soldier beetle; wasp beetle; brassy pollen beetle; thick-legged flower beetle; hover fly – Scaeva pyrastri; a field grasshopper; an orb-web spider, a slug and a snail. The six bumble bees include: Bombus lapidarius, B. pratorum, B. agrorum and three Bombus lucorum. The butterflies are: small skipper, gatekeeper and clouded yellow.

on plant debris and fungi. Woodlice feed on deep litter where the lower layers are damp; they are terrestrial members of the crab family and most of the species have to keep their bodies damp, as their skin is so thin that they can easily dry out and die. In the marshy soil of water meadows, woodlice take the place of earthworms in breaking down plant debris.

In the secrecy of darkness, millipedes feed on decaying vegetation; some of them also eat small carrion, such as dead snails. Centipedes hunt in the litter layer by night, too; they stalk unwary insects, spiders, slugs and any other invertebrates they are able to tackle. They kill by injecting poison through a pair of special fangs.

Earwigs are nocturnal insects which feed on tender foliage. The female earwig lays about 40 eggs in a soil cavity in early spring; she stays with the eggs, guarding them until they hatch. The earwig nymphs are fed and tended by their mother until they are able to fend for themselves; you may come across a family group in the spring. I once inadvertently scattered some earwig eggs by sweeping them out of the crevice in which the mother earwig was guarding them. The earwig set about collecting the eggs up again, and wasn't satisfied until she had gathered together all the eggs that she and I could find.

There are a number of animals living in the soil whose larvae feed on the roots of grasses and crops. Many beetles are useful, being members of the decomposer team. Some are carnivorous and feed on invertebrates, but two beetles at least have very destructive larvae – the click beetle and the cockchafer beetle, whose larvae are wireworms and white grubs respectively. Wireworms are thin yellow-brown grubs whose skin is very tough, hence their name; these larvae stay in the soil, feeding for up to five years. White grubs are a rather dirty white in colour, and live in the soil for two or three years until they have become fully grown fat larvae about 4 cm (1½ in) long, curved into a sickle shape.

Some crane flies – daddy-long-legs – have destructive larvae, too; these are known as leatherjackets. They are dirty brown, legless grubs with very tough skins; when the grubs are fully grown they pupate in the soil and the crane fly drags itself out of the ground in autumn.

You will often see birds strutting about a field, they are usually looking for – or listening for – larvae. Wireworms are taken by gulls, pheasants, rooks and starlings, as well as some predacious beetles. White grubs are enjoyed by gulls, rooks and starlings; hedgehogs and moles savour them too. Leatherjackets are eaten by rooks, starlings, blackbirds and thrushes.

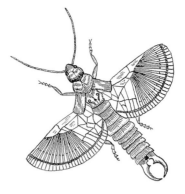

Earwigs have lacy wings folded away beneath their tiny wing cases. It must take them quite a while to fold up the wings neatly & tuck them away again – no wonder they seldom fly.

This is a crane fly or daddy-long-legs. The hind wings of true flies are reduced to pin-like organs called halteres, which act as gyroscopes & help to maintain stability in flight.

The larvae of some moths, such as the flounced rustic and grass moth, also feed on grass roots; while the caterpillars of other moths and butterflies feed on the leaf blades of grasses and, where there are flowers, the adults stay around to sip nectar. Look out for various species of skippers and graylings, as well as gatekeeper, ringlet, meadow brown, wall and small heath butterflies and lesser yellow underwing, dark archer and drinker moths.

The hammock web spider hangs its hammock-like web between grass stems, while the purse web spider uses a buried silk tube as a lair. The spider sits patiently in its lair, waiting for an insect to become snared in the fine mesh of a finger-like extension. Crab spiders wait on flowers, their colour gradually changing to merge with their background. When an unsuspecting insect visits the flower, the crab spider seizes its prey. I have seen a crab spider take a honey bee in this way: the shock tactics were so effective that the spider was in no danger from the bee's sting.

Where animals have been grazing, the faeces are dealt with by earthworms, dung beetles and fly larvae. Earthworms feed directly on droppings and usually discharge their wastes below the soil surface, so playing an important part in mixing dung with the soil. More earthworms live in grassland soils than in arable land; this is because there is more food for them in grassland and they are not disturbed by cultivation activities. Earthworm burrows are channels along which water can drain away from the surface; air is able to filter through the burrows, and thicker plant roots grow along them. Worm casts enrich the surface soil, as they are well mixed with organic material which makes them rich in plant foods.

Some dung beetles lay their eggs in the dung of horses, cattle and sheep; others, like dor beetles, dig burrows in the soil, then carry down plugs of dung which are stored in brood chambers off the main shaft. Eggs are laid close by this stored food, so the newly hatched larvae don't have to move far. The male and female horned dung beetle, *Copris lunaris*, work together to excavate a burrow under cow dung, and both adults care for the larvae until they are ready to pupate.

The animals around cowpats will be mainly beetles and flies; there will be fly and beetle larvae in some of the pats, and you will see where birds have been pecking the larvae out. The golden dung fly is usually very much in evidence; this insect lays eggs in the dung where the larvae feed and mature. Some of the insects around the cowpat are predators who hunt the scavengers. Now you probably feel like washing your hands!

Cowslips are flowers of rich, calcareous grasslands. They are visited by long-tongued insects such as this bee-fly, whose long-haired body resembles that of a bee.

Crab spiders wait for flower visitors - then they pounce.

MOLES: MINERS PAR EXCELLENCE

Molehills are a familiar sight in open grassland; the 'tumps' of rich brown earth look like small, newly dug graves. I like to call moles by their old name, 'mouldewarp', which is from the Saxon 'molde', meaning earth, and 'warpen', to throw.

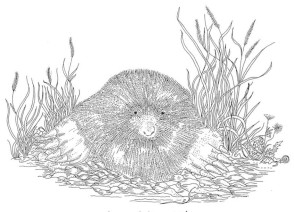

'mouldewarp'

A mole spends most of its life in solitude, patrolling its underground burrow system or digging to extend the burrow system and find more food. Moles dislike all other moles; they are very bad-tempered and aggressive animals. There is a truce between the sexes during the mating period; a peace treaty is also honoured between a mother and her young, but only for about a month while they are suckling, after which they are driven from the nest to fend for themselves.

The small black earthworkers are well adapted to their underground life. The spade-like forefeet each have five long, pointed claws, able to dig through the hardest soil. The strong shoulder joints are set well forward on the body, so the mole is able to dig in front of its nose. The hairs of the silky black fur are all about the same length and are non-directional, so the mole can go backwards or forwards in tight-fitting tunnels without difficulty. Their tails have sensitive hairs to detect obstacles when the mole is backing in a tunnel, and their noses are studded with tiny capsules called Eimer's organs, which perceive temperature, humidity and pressure – they also turn bright red with excitement. Moles' eyes are tiny, but good enough to be able to detect motion and shades of light. Their ears are internal; their hearing is not acute but the sensitive tail hairs and a fringe of stiff hairs on the edge of the forepaws pick up soil-borne vibrations.

In soft soil a mole 'swims', using a breaststroke technique. When digging in firmer soil it uses one forefoot at a time, bracing its body against the sides of the tunnel while digging. A molehill is the loose soil that has been excavated during tunnel construction. The mole digs a vertical shaft to the surface and pushes the excess soil up and out at the top.

Moles feed on soil invertebrates and sometimes on surface carrion. If I find a small dead animal I usually put it under an old wire tray to watch the action of the decomposers. Last summer the bodies of voles, shrews and mice kept disappearing, and I couldn't think who was taking them. Then one day, while I was watching a ladybird coming out of pupation, out of the corner of my eye I saw a mole 'swim' out of the ground, squeeze through the wire and 'bodysnatch' a vole! Later I spread some sand around the bodies that I found, and it was

Hogweed or cow parsnip, Heracleum
hondylium, is a common roadside
bellifer which flowers for most of
mmer and early autumn. Many
visit the large umbels of flowers
listen with nectar.

always mole feet that were imprinted in the sand. Earthworms are usually the mole's main diet; they may be stored in cavities along the tunnels, rendered immobile by having their heads bitten off.

I have made friends with many animals, but I think the strangest one of all was a mole. We met in June 1981; I was walking past a flower bed when out came a young mole and put his front paws on my foot. He stuck his little nose in the air and waved it around as though he was making sure that he had found the right person. I carefully put my hand down – moles have sharp teeth – but he came into my hand and I picked him up. This seemed to please him, and he pressed his head into my hand to be stroked.

Green woodpeckers are often seen on the ground, where they enjoy eating ants and their larvae.

The visitors to the Countryside Centre were delighted to see a mole at such close quarters and amused at the way he appeared when I walked by 'his' flower bed. But I was afraid that one of the cats would damage this unusually friendly creature, so one evening, when I was taking a party on a guided walk on the moor, we took mole along too and left him in what I thought would be a good place. To my great surprise, the next day mole was back in the garden waiting for me! We took him on two more guided walks, leaving him in good 'mole places' each time, but still he came back to the garden. This peculiar behaviour intrigued me and I had to find out what was behind it, so I spent some time watching mole very carefully. He seemed to have a problem; he would dig a hole, put his head and the front part of his body into it and there he would stay, apparently unaware that his little rear end was sticking out of the hole for all to see. Out he would come and dig another hole and stick his head into that one; he must have found enough earthworms in the warm, damp, well-manured soil to keep him fed, probably supplementing his diet with invertebrates from among the plants. But, I thought, he will have to find his true habitat before the weather turns dry and the earthworms go deeper into the soil. So I dug a deep hole in the garden and pushed a pole along and through the soil as far as I could in various directions. The next time mole came to greet me, I showed him the passages I'd made. It was a fine game! I put him into a tunnel and he waddled along it, then turned round and came back. Fortunately he found plenty of food along those tunnels and he left us.

ENIGMATIC ANTS

Meadow ants spend most of their time underground, and they are responsible for the grass-covered mounds which may often be seen in meadows.

'Emmet' is an ancient name for ant and some people call the meadow ant's mounds 'emmet casts'. These mounds may be a nuisance to the farmer during hay-making, but the ants improve the quality of the pasture by mixing the soil and aerating it. The mounds made by yellow meadow ants are elongated, with a long slope up to the highest point and a steeper slope which faces east or south-east. The ants live in the eastern end of the mound, possibly because it is drier and receives the warmth of the morning sun.

All ants are social in habit and, like the honey bees, their colonies endure from one year to another. The ants themselves are long-lived; worker ants are known to live up to seven years and the queens up to fifteen.

Their feeding habits vary. Some species are carnivorous, feeding on insects and other small animals, dead or alive; others are vegetarians, eating seeds, fungi or honeydew.

Ants have the same mechanism of sex determination as wasps and bees, so fertilized eggs produce females and eggs which are not fertilized produce males. At the height of summer, there are three different castes living in an ant's nest, all presided over by their mother, a wingless queen. The largest are queens, who have four thin, transparent wings; the smallest are males; and the intermediate-sized ants are the workers, the only ants easily seen in the nest during the rest of the year. The workers are wingless females which are not sexually developed, although they can sometimes lay eggs.

On a warm, humid afternoon or evening in summer, male and female ants emerge from their nests over a wide area. No one really knows what triggers them off, or how the different nests synchronize their flights, but I suspect that temperature and humidity have a lot to do with it. The ants usually make for a conspicuous object on the landscape, and gather in large numbers around it. Birds are quick to detect the swarming ants, and chase and devour many of the insects as they take part in their nuptial flights. Mating takes place in the air, often between ants from different nests, which is a good thing as it prevents inbreeding; when mating has taken place, the pairs drop down to the ground, where the males soon During her marriage flight, the queen receives insects h sperm to last her a lifetime; and, as I said, this which go up to fifteen years!

Queen ants shed their wings at a preformed abscission point near the wing base because they will not need them again.

The mated females tear off their wings, as they won't be needed again. Then the ants have a choice; a queen will either return to her old nest – for ants will tolerate more than one queen – or the newly mated queen will find a suitable place to overwinter. It must be a miserable time for a young queen ant, sealed up until spring and living on the food reserves in her body and on the degenerating wing muscles that she no longer needs.

During this winter period, the new queen's eggs have been maturing, and in spring she begins to lay, feeding the larvae on her own saliva. As soon as the young worker ants become adult, they take over the building and management of the nest, and the queen's activities are reduced to egg-laying.

Life in the colony centres on the queen; she remains in her chamber laying eggs and being tended by the workers. She is fed on sugar-rich regurgitated fluid which is gathered from flowers as nectar or as honeydew from aphids. The tiny eggs are carried away from the royal chamber to nurseries elsewhere in the nest, where the larvae are fed on sweet fluid and insect grubs; they are taken from room to room as they grow. When the larvae pupate they are kept near the surface of the nest; here they have the benefit of the warmth of the sun which helps them to mature quickly. This is why, when we lift up a stone or log, we see ants picking up white 'eggs' and scurrying away in a sort of organized chaos. The 'eggs' are the pupating larvae; these are the 'ants' eggs' which are sold as fish food.

Ant colonies are very stable and long-lasting, with a good community spirit. The great success of ants stems mainly from the versatility of their diet and the flexibility of their behaviour. The workers feed the larvae on partly chewed and predigested food; the larvae produce drops of fluid and saliva which the workers like, so they continually lick and caress the larvae. The workers exchange food, too, and information is constantly being passed around, with much head-rubbing and antennae-knocking.

When ants go off on a hunting trip, they keep track of their direction from the nest by noting the position of the sun; if there is no sun then they are able to use polarized light as bees do. When one ant has found a good food supply and returned to the nest, other workers follow the same route, scurrying along the track in both directions and following the scent left by the others.

The herding instinct of some ants stems from their love of sweet fluids and especially honeydew; this is the sap of plants sucked by aphids who excrete the surplus in the form of a sweet sticky fluid. Ants treat the aphids

The queen lays a pile of eggs & tends the brood, living on the reserves in her redundant flight muscles & feeding the larvae on a salivary secretion.

The new ant colony begins to function. The eggs, larvae & pupae are piled in neatly sorted heaps in different chambers of the nest.

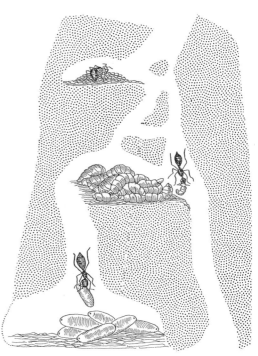

90

near to their colony rather like cows; they are guarded from predators and 'milked'. The ant strokes the aphid's rear end with its antennae; this stimulates the aphid into secreting a drop of honeydew which the ant eats and later regurgitates to feed to the queen or the larvae.

The yellow meadow ant keeps herds of aphids in the nest, where they are 'stabled' on the roots of plants that hang from above into the nest cavity. Here they feed on sap from the roots and are 'milked' regularly. During the winter, batches of aphid eggs are stored and protected until spring.

The large blue butterfly has an interesting relationship with ants. The female butterfly deposits her eggs on thyme leaves and, when they hatch, the little caterpillars feed on the flower buds and any of their smaller kin they may encounter. After the caterpillar's second moult, a gland develops on the seventh segment of the body and a sweet smell is exuded. Ants are attracted to the smell and they begin to tend the caterpillar. After the third moult, the caterpillar abandons the food plant and creeps about on the ground, arching its swollen back. This behaviour stimulates the ants and they approach the caterpillar, who hunches its body up, making it easy for the ants to pick it up and carry it back to the nest. The ants feed the caterpillar on mature ant larvae and guard it from predators and parasites; they stroke the caterpillar's back with their forelegs and antennae, so inducing the gland to distend and release drops of sweet fluid. In late spring, the caterpillar, fat with ant larvae, goes into pupation; a month later, the butterfly emerges. What consternation! The ants don't want this intruder in their nest and they chase the butterfly; fortunately it is covered with downy scales and when the ants bite at the butterfly they are left with jaws full of scales.

The blue butterfly caterpillar is totally dependent on ants for its protection and food; if the pasture in which the ants live is ploughed up and the ants disappear, then so do the large blue butterflies.

Ants have large heads & one or two 'waists' (petioles), where part of the abdomen is constricted behind the thorax.

Ants' antennae have a bend in the middle, like an elbow.

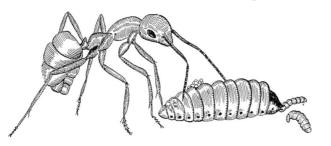

ant 'milking' an aphid

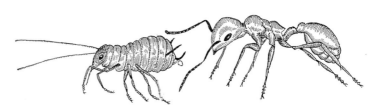

ant 'milking' a large blue butterfly larva

INSECTS ON THE HOP
Grasshoppers and Crickets

One of the joys of lying in a meadow, watching and listening, is the constant 'chirping' of grasshoppers; the game is trying to spot them!

Grasshoppers and crickets belong to the order Orthoptera, a word which means straight-winged and refers to the narrow forewings which lie along the sides of the body of the insect.

Bush crickets have long antennae – often longer than the body – and are sometimes called long-horned grasshoppers. The females have broad, sabre-like ovipositors and are thus easily differentiated from the males. Bush crickets are partly carnivorous and, as their name suggests, they are often found in bushes or in taller herbage than grasshoppers.

Male bush crickets sing by rubbing their wing bases together. It is a file and scraper mechanism, like drawing a comb over a card; the file is on the left forewing while the hind edge of the right forewing forms the scraper. The sounds are picked up by tiny drum-like membranes, tympanal organs, on the front legs.

Grasshoppers have short antennae and are sometimes called short-horned grasshoppers, which distinguishes them from bush crickets. Grasshoppers are vegetarian, eating leaves and grass, and are usually found in low-growing vegetation where the adults chirp merrily, rubbing the row of pegs on the inner side of the large thigh against the prominent veins of the forewing on each side. Each species has its own particular song; the males call stridently while the females have a quieter chirp. Grasshopper 'ears' are at the base of the first abdominal segment on each side of the body.

Most grasshoppers and crickets have one generation a year; the egg is the overwintering stage. The eggs of crickets are laid singly, while those of grasshoppers are laid in groups, surrounded by a pod of earth mixed with a glandular secretion.

The young insect, a nymph, is creamy white and enclosed in a thin, transparent sac. During late spring the nymph wriggles out of the sac, sheds its skin and emerges as a tiny wingless replica of the adult. As the nymph feeds and grows, it becomes too big for its skin and has to moult. The number of instars varies between species. After each moult, the little grasshopper is larger and a stage nearer to becoming an adult. There is no pupation stage in this form of development, which is called incomplete metamorphosis. After the final moult the insect is a mature adult, ready to reproduce.

Hind end of grasshopper abdomen

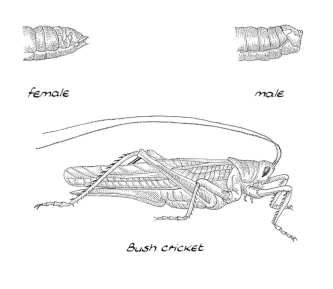

female

male

Bush cricket

Wavy hair grass

Females have a broad, sabre-like ovipositor, & so are easily distinguished from the male.

male

female

HOVER FLIES: THE MINICOPTERS

As well as the many bees which visit meadow flowers, there are some insects which also pollinate flowers and look like small bees, but are really flies in disguise. These are hover flies.

Watch a hover fly as it hovers over a flower. The wings are a blur; they vibrate rapidly at well over a hundred times a second, moving in a flat figure-of-eight, while the head remains perfectly still in relation to the thorax. When it lands, look at its velvety livery and the size and colour of those large eyes which often meet above the head. Should you find a dead hover fly, take a close look at it; behind the pair of wings you will see two little knobs where another pair of wings would fit. The hind wings of true flies have become highly modified into a pair of club-shaped balancing organs called halteres. During flight the halteres vibrate up and down at the same time as the wings, until the speed of the vibration is such that they act like tiny gyroscopes to control flight movement.

Look at halteres on other true flies; the crane fly (daddy-long-legs) is a good example.

Opposite. *Work from the bottom of this picture and you will find: an egg pod, a vermiform larva, four instar nymphs, a discarded skin and an adult grasshopper.*

93

Hover flies have mouth parts that mop up liquid food. It takes a great deal of energy to fly so well, and the best fuel available is nectar. They do take pollen, too, as both sexes need protein in order to become sexually mature.

When hover flies visit flowers, they can be seen very easily by birds and other predators, so it is not surprising that they mimic other frequent flower visitors. Bees and wasps are avoided by many predators because they are able to sting; the predators recognize the dark brown or black and yellow colour combination and avoid any insect with livery in those colours, so the hover fly is reasonably safe.

Many hover flies have carnivorous larvae that eat aphids, making them doubly important insects to have around. Here is the life-cycle of one such hover fly, *Syrphus ribesii*.

Male hover flies congregate and wait for a passing female; the fastest and most agile male will get to the female first, and mating takes place. Female hover flies are attracted to aphid colonies by the smell of honeydew on the plant leaves; here the female will lay one or two eggs, then fly off to find another colony and lay more.

After three or four days the eggs hatch and out come the pale larvae. They are blind, legless and soft-bodied, but their mouth parts are sharp; the head casts round in a semicircle, rearing up and down until it contacts an aphid. Then the mouth parts grip and pierce the aphid's skin and the sweet, sap-filled body fluids are sucked into the hover fly larva's body. The larva moults its skin three times during its ten days' growth, during which time it will probably have consumed the contents of hundreds of aphids. Pupation takes place on a leaf or twig; the pupa case is brown and pear-shaped, and protects the insect for the ten days or so that it is in pupation.

There are several generations of hover flies through the summer; then in autumn the larvae find hiding places in the soil where they overwinter, not pupating until spring is well advanced.

Not all hover fly species are flower visitors; some are predators and others are scavengers.

Hover fly, Syrphus ribesii. *Note the halteres behind the wings.*

The mouth parts mop up liquid food.

Hover flies fly backwards, forwards, upwards, downwards and sideways. The energy fuel used is nectar.

A PLACE TO HIDE

There are some animals which live among the grass stems, using them as cover and homes as well as food.

The tiniest, daintiest mammal to be found among the grass stems is the harvest mouse. This acrobatic rodent weighs so little that it is able to climb amongst the grass stalks without weighing them down.

As its name implies, the harvest mouse has always been associated with cornfields. However, reaping machines and combine harvesters, shortly followed by the plough, have driven the harvest mouse to the field edges, where the grass is long at the base of the hedge. My observations suggest that the crop of standing corn is still used for nesting and feeding in early summer, after which the mice retreat to the safety of the field edges.

The harvest mouse shreds the leaves of grasses without separating them from the stalk – so the nest is woven around a living framework of four or five stems. The small round nest is only 7.5 cm (3 in) in diameter, and is built about 50 cm (20 in) above the ground, where it sways with the stem. Here it gently rocks the half-dozen or so babies in their bed of chewed grass and thistledown.

In winter, harvest mice must take care to keep warm and they nest in old shallow burrows or under tussocks of grass. They have to eat their own body weight of food every day and so are active by day and night, feeding on seeds, fruit, green shoots and insects. The mice themselves are eaten by rooks, crows, pheasants, kestrels, buzzards, owls, large toads, stoats, weasels and foxes; not surprisingly, harvest mice have a short life expectancy.

Field voles differ from bank voles in having a longer body, a shorter tail and dark brown fur. These voles enjoy living in overgrown fields with rough tussocky grass – we have lots in our wild garden, and I hear them defending their territories aggressively with loud squeals and long chattering arguments with any other vole who dares to cross the invisible boundary lines. There is a log under which a field vole nests and, on the rare occasions when I peep underneath, I see the nest chamber, larder and latrine, with a runway system extending out to the surrounding grass area.

Grass is the vole's main food, but they will also eat bulbs, roots and tree roots at ground level. They are out and about by day and night, so all their predators are attracted to the field.

By day hares rest close to the ground, in grass or in a furrow where they are easily overlooked. There are few hares about now, but you may be lucky enough to see

Tormentil

95

them early in the morning or in the dusk. Hares are larger than rabbits; the adults have long powerful legs which enable them to sprint at 65 kph (40 mph). It is a strange way of running, as the hind legs push so far forward that they land in front of the forelegs in a peculiar leap-frog motion. Hare ears are long and black-tipped, and the hare's wild eyes are set high on the head to give an almost all round view.

Acorns

Hares have solitary lives, but produce three or four litters between midwinter and late summer. A buck will guard a doe who is almost in season, but if he becomes too excited the doe, who is larger than the buck, threatens him by rising up on to her haunches and punching out at him if he tries to get too near too soon. Some males get carried away in their enthusiasm and lunge back at the female, and so they start boxing; other males in the area smell the odour of the female and are drawn to the fight, hoping to claim the female when it is over. The scene looks like a boxing match, with two adversaries and a ring of spectators!

Leverets – baby hares – are born in the open field. At birth they have a full coat of red-brown fur, their eyes are open and they are fully mobile. Although the mother hare has two or three babies, after the first day or so they are kept in separate forms within her territory; a form is a slight depression in the ground. The babies come together just after sunset each day to feed from their mother; they are weaned early and when they are a month old they feed entirely on vegetation. Baby hares are very vulnerable; they are often killed by farm machinery and by insecticide spray, while weedkillers destroy plants needed by the hares for a nutritious diet. Their natural enemies are foxes and stoats.

Unlike hares, rabbits live together in large, sociable groups. They are able to alter the ecology of the area in which they live by persistently nibbling grass and other plants down to ground level, until they are eventually replaced by moss, which rabbits don't eat. They do, however, often eat young trees in their first year of growth and this can prevent regeneration within a woodland. Rabbits will eat the bottom branches of trees which grow close to the ground, and in bad weather they strip the bark from mature trees to nibble the sweet cambium layer beneath.

When rabbit populations build up to high numbers, the rabbit flea which carries the myxomatosis virus spreads amongst the families and many rabbits die. Since this dreadful disease was introduced from the Continent in 1953, some rabbits have developed an immunity to it, but it does still kill many baby rabbits.

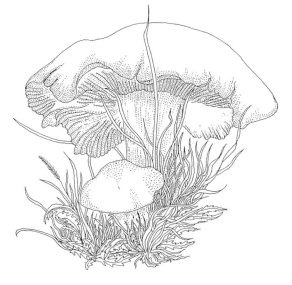

St. George's mushroom

Rabbits live in warrens, which are complicated networks of tunnels, enlarged in places to form resting spaces and nursery chambers. Nest chambers deep in the centre of the warren are taken by the dominant females, while those females who are low on the matriarchal ladder have shallow chambers near to the surface. The breeding season is from the middle of winter to late summer; in one season a female is able to produce up to 30 offspring, each of which is able to breed within four months. This is quite a feat considering the babies are born blind, naked and helpless and are only fed once a day. The warrens used to be situated in open fields, but this is no longer desirable because of frequent cultivation and deep ploughing; so rabbits now tend to live under hedgerows and along field edges, making dawn and dusk sorties into the field to feed. Rabbits are taken by many predators, including foxes, stoats, weasels and man.

The skylark rises high into the air, sweetly warbling its way upwards and back again down to earth. These birds live in farmland, grassland, meadow and duneland areas, where they eat seeds, insects and insect larvae.

Skylarks nest in hollows on the ground, often partly concealed by a tussock of grass. The eggs are off-white to pale green with brown or olive speckles, so they are well camouflaged. The stripy chicks are difficult to see, too, as they stay in the thick ground cover for protection until they are about three weeks old, when they are able to fly.

Pheasants live in my wild garden and in the surrounding fields; they forage for seeds, insects, small mammals and tiny frogs, and in spring they peck at any green shoot that appears.

The cock pheasant has a harem of several females which he protects from other cock pheasants; but he is a coward when any other threat arises. The nest is little more than a shallow scrape in the ground and the eggs are buff coloured; the chicks are well camouflaged with mottled fawn and black. Some cock pheasants have a white ring around their neck, some are pale gold, some russet and others olive green.

We bought a pair of quails once – just to watch for a while, after which we liberated them. They are rather like tiny partridges, only 18 cm (7 in) long, with a liquid call 'whit-whit-whit', which seems to come from anywhere but the quail's bill.

Quails are streaked down the back and on the head and neck, so they blend in well with the grasses of cornfields and hayfields. The female makes a depression in grass where she puts her brown-blotched cream eggs; the chicks are striped, which helps to conceal them as they lie low in the grass.

The drab-coloured skylark has a wonderful, warbling song.

Hedgerow Ecology

Why are so many hedges still being grubbed out? I mourn the disappearance of any hedge and fail to see the desirability of enormous fields, especially when we have European food mountains. Oh yes, I see how much easier it is to manoeuvre a giant machine around a large field; but then comes the crop sprayer killing every living creature around – including the ones that do good. A hedgerow is home to many animals, including those who would rid a smaller field of its pests. Happily more and more people, including farmers, are beginning to share this view and when I see a new hedge being planted, or an old one being brought back to life, that is a cause for rejoicing.

It is worth watching the changes in the flower population along a hedgerow as the seasons progress. Some species go out of bloom while others are opening their petals, giving us a cavalcade of colour and beauty against the secret teeming backdrop of the hedge itself: a backdrop that is fresh green in spring, dark and apparently still in summer, glowing with fruits of all kinds in autumn and rustling with sheltering birds in winter; but always full of life.

Bilberries

WHAT IS A HEDGE?

A hedge may be a low stone wall, a high turfed bank surmounted by shrubs, or a bank of osiers marking the boundary of water and fields. But for most people, a hedge is a line of shrubs about 1.5 metres (5 ft) high and 1–2 metres (3–6 ft) wide, forming the boundary of a field, a roadside or a garden.

An unmanaged hedge soon becomes overgrown and begins to look like a long narrow wood. This is the way many hedges probably looked when the early farmers began to clear the forests to make large open spaces in which to grow their crops and keep cattle. The trees were cut down with stone axes, or ring-barked by having a circle cut deeply around the trunk to kill them; 2 or 3 metres (5–10 ft) width of forest was left standing to mark the boundaries of a domain. When the cleared area was very large, it may have been divided into fields; the growing and grazing areas would be cleared of stones, which were then piled along the dividing lines forming low walls. Some of the field boundaries were probably made of live stakes or brush wood; it would be sensible for farmers wishing to keep domestic animals in, and wild animals out, to use a thorny barrier such as hawthorn. A few of the stakes and twigs probably rooted; and, as hawthorn grows quickly, there would soon be a living barrier. When shrubs were seen to work well as a barrier, as well as being a good source of kindling and berries, the hedge would undoubtedly have become very popular.

I don't think that the habits of cattle and sheep have changed much over the centuries; they seem to go through life with a fixation about the other side of the hedge, and they will work at any small gap until they can push through it. So it must always have been in the farmer's interest to keep the hedge thick and strong by cutting and laying. The craft of maintaining hedges has been recorded in books and papers on farming from the eleventh century onwards; disputes about the removal of particular hedgerows are recorded from the thirteenth century onward.

The word 'hedge' was added to the names of a number of plants and animals commonly found in that habitat: hedge parsley, hedge woundwort, hedge garlic, hedge bindweed; hedgehog, hedge sparrow (dunnock) and hedge brown butterfly. These names have been used since medieval times.

A hedgerow is a long corridor along which many animals and plants spread themselves out across the countryside, linking one fragment of woodland with

carbon dioxide and water
the sun's energy and chlorophyll
produce carbohydrates and oxygen

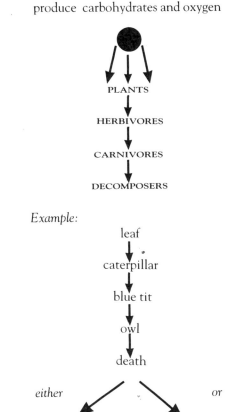

Example:

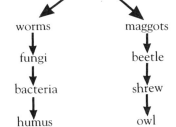

recycled

another. In this way, the plants and animals of the
ancient woodlands have not been entirely lost. Over the
centuries, many plants and animals have gradually
adapted to the man-made countryside; it is possible that
in the new pattern of copses, fields, hedgerows, gardens
and houses some wildlife may have become even more
successful. For example, birds such as the robin,
blackbird and thrush could be more common now than
when they lived in a purely woodland habitat; while the
seed-eating chaffinch, yellowhammer and greenfinch
must find more food in a field of corn or stubble than
they ever did in the ancient woodlands.

Blackberries

Hedgerows are particularly rich habitats for wildlife
because they combine the features of a woodland with
those of open fields; while a hedge with a ditch and bank
is often home to plants and animals once more usually
found in habitats which are rapidly disappearing, such as
marshland and old pasture.

The constant growth and annual cutting of a hedge
means that the habitat continually changes, encouraging
a great diversity of species. A lot depends on when the
hedge is cut, as a matter of a few weeks can greatly
influence the floral composition and the insects who
depend on the hedgerow.

As you walk along a hedgerow, the insects and spiders
may not be immediately apparent. Stand and watch
quietly; when the animals feel safe you will see
movement. As your eyes become 'tuned in' to the shapes
and shadows, you will probably be surprised at what you see.

No animal is safe; there are predators everywhere. If
an animal is seen, heard or smelt, it is in potential
danger. But animals must feed and reproduce
successfully, so defensive strategies have to be adopted.
Each species has its own strategies, and these are adapted
to its environment and to the other animals with which
it interacts. Many of the insects you will find are
coloured to merge in with the background. Some are red
and black or yellow and black; these showy warning
colours make the insects easily recognized by predators
who have probably eaten one of these bright creatures
before, and have found them to taste horrid or, in the
case of wasps, to sting fiercely. So the insects with
warning colours are largely left alone. There are insects
who deceive predators by displaying false warning
colours; the wasp beetle models its colours and antennae
movements on those of the common wasp. Look out for
flies who mimic wasps and bees; remember that flies have
only two wings.

A look at the sections of a hedgerow will give some
idea of the diversity of life to be found there.

Hover fly

THE HAWTHORN

Hawthorn, or quickthorn, *Crataegus monogyna*, is a tree of glades and woodland edges where it grows to about 12 metres (40 ft) in height. It is probably the most common hedgerow plant; the word for hedge is based on the Saxon name for the fruit of the hawthorn – hag or haw. So you will find haga (Anglo-Saxon), hagan (Old German), Hecke (modern German), haie (modern French) and hege (Old English), all meaning hedge.

About 150 insects are associated with the hawthorn; these insects will also visit other plants in the family Rosaceae which grow along the hedgerow. Hawthorn flowers produce nectar and attract flies, beetles and various bees in late spring. Of the many insects found in association with hawthorn, 80 or more are moth larvae; it is fortunate that they are able to eat other plants, too, or the hawthorn would be defoliated regularly!

The looper caterpillars of the winter moth *Operophtera brumata* hatch in the middle of spring and eat young leaves and flower buds voraciously in the protective shelter of leaves woven together with silk. The silk shimmers with a silver sheen and last year I saw a tree so draped with the webs of looper caterpillars that from a distance it appeared to have been sprayed with silver. The caterpillars are usually fully grown by late spring and they fall to the ground to pupate in the soil; much to the relief of the trees, I should think. The moths emerge in late autumn and winter; the females only have vestigial wings and are unable to fly, so they climb up the tree and sit on the bark waiting for a male. Fruit growers fasten greased bands round the trunks of their trees to stop the female moths climbing up and laying their eggs among the leaf buds.

Chinese character moths, *Cilix glaucata*, are so called because they have small white markings on the forewings very like Chinese script. When the moths are at rest they resemble bird droppings, so they are left alone.

Lappet moths, *Gastropacha quercifolia*, are also well camouflaged; they look like brown leaves. Small eggar caterpillars live in large communities, sheltering in a silken web by day and leaving it to feed at night.

Yellow-tail moths, *Euproctis similis*, are white furry insects with a tail of yellow irritant hairs. When the female moth lays her eggs, the large batches are protected by a covering of hairs taken from her tail. The caterpillars are hairy, too, and, when pupation takes place, the brown cocoon can be seen to incorporate some of the larval hairs.

In winter you may find the oblong brown pupa cases of

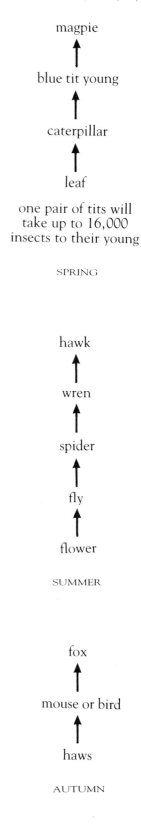

Food chain – yearly cycle

magpie

↑

blue tit young

↑

caterpillar

↑

leaf

one pair of tits will
take up to 16,000
insects to their young

SPRING

hawk

↑

wren

↑

spider

↑

fly

↑

flower

SUMMER

fox

↑

mouse or bird

↑

haws

AUTUMN

(continued overleaf)

101

the hawthorn sawfly fastened on the twigs. This sawfly measures about 4 mm (⅙ in) across its wings. Sawflies have four wings, so they are not true flies; they are members of the wasp, bee and ant family, Hymenoptera. Sawfly larvae are meticulous defoliators; the larvae can be identified as sawfly as they have *more than* five pairs of abdominal, or clasping, legs. The caterpillars of butterflies and moths have *no more than* five pairs of clasping legs.

Hawthorn berries are eaten by birds and by small mammals who live in the hedge bottom. Birds nest in the hawthorn, use it as a roost and hunt among the spiky branches. These birds and small mammals are hunted by birds of prey, foxes, stoats and weasels. Shrews hunt for invertebrates on the hedge bank. Most predators leave shrews alone, not liking the smell extruded from their stink glands; but owls take them, so they must not mind the smell.

The hawthorn shield bug also eats the berries in autumn and the young leaves in spring. Another interesting member of this family is the parent bug, who sits over her diamond-shaped egg batch until they hatch, and then actively continues to protect the young. If a predator approaches the family, the mother hustles the youngsters under a leaf, then acts as a decoy herself.

Pied shield bugs are found on white dead nettle, and on other leaves in the family Labiatae along the hedge bottom. White dead nettle has nettle-shaped leaves, but does not have stinging hairs. The flowers are visited by long-tongued bumble bees who collect the nectar.

Cuckoo pint gently traps tiny flies in its lower chamber, releasing them when pollination has taken place. It has the name 'cuckoo' because it opens at the time of the year that the cuckoo returns to lay eggs, very often in the nests of those shy hedgerow birds, the dunnocks. Cuckoo spit can also be found at this time. This is a secretion from the nymph of the froghopper bug, who doesn't want to be either roasted by the sun or eaten by a bird; the sticky froth is a protection from both.

Bluebells on a hedge bank indicate that this was a piece of old woodland. The flowers are pollinated by bees and bee flies; bee flies are true flies who look like fat bees. Stitchwort and red campion are woodland plants which are often found along a hedgerow; foxgloves are plants of woodland edges and glades, which are pollinated by bumble bees.

owl

↑

shrew

↑

beetle
(eats pupae)

↑

looper
caterpillars

↑

leaf

WINTER

caterpillars may escape the birds in spring but other predators wait

Hawthorn berries

102

This picture has 38 animals to spot.
From left to right & starting at the top, find:
bumble bee, solitary bee, common flower bug, kestrel with mouse, blackbird,
hover fly, crab spider, sawfly larva, lackey moth & caterpillar,
honey bee, sawfly, small ermine caterpillars, blue tit & winter moth larva,
common capsid bug, magpie stealing an egg from a chaffinch nest,
greenfly, mirid bug, dunnock nest, snipe-fly, seven-spot ladybird, orb web spider,
great tit, early moth & larva, small eggar & larva, leaf beetle, male & female winter moth,
hawthorn shield bug, snail, wood mouse, leaf hopper,
slug, dunnock with crane-fly, hedgehog & bank vole.

GOAT WILLOW

The sallow or goat willow, *Salix caprea*, grows to about 15 metres (50 ft). These willows are not dependent on water-logged ground. They are dioecious, having all male flowers on one tree and female flowers on another. The female flowers or catkins are silky, grey-green structures, soft to the touch and giving the trees their other popular name of 'pussy willow'. The male flowers are fat and grey, with a halo of golden stamens.

Goat willow leaf beginning to turn

Bee-keepers used to plant goat willows close to their hives, as the abundant nectar and pollen gives a good food source early in the year. Nectar is the fuel, the energy supply, of many insects, while pollen is for growth; both are very important. Honey bees are glad of the food in spring as their winter food stores are diminishing; queen bumble bees depend on a good food supply when they come out of hibernation and need to build up their strength for the labours ahead. Willow trees have about 260 insects associated with them.

Willow sawfly larvae and eyed hawkmoth larvae often strip whole sprays of leaves from the trees. The purple emperor butterfly lays eggs on sallow in summer; this is a high-flying butterfly attracted to dung and carrion. The puss moth lays her eggs on sallow; puss moth caterpillars not only deter would-be predators by raising their colourful heads and waving their red tail filaments, but they also eject an acid spray from a gland behind the head. They pupate in a cocoon of chewed bark lined with silk which is attached to the tree trunk; moths emerge in late spring. Someone once asked me to look after a puss moth caterpillar that was due to go into pupation. I agreed to care for it, but asked why they didn't want to watch the process. 'Because it bites,' was the answer! A caterpillar who chews up bark to make a cocoon does have sharp jaws, so keep your fingers out of the way, or they may be mistaken for twigs.

Galls are often found on willows; particularly red bean galls, which erupt on the leaves. The goat willow often has a very attractive terminal gall on its shoots; it is called a camellia gall and it looks like a green rosette. The structure is of 30 to 60 shortened leaves all crowded together and measuring around 8 cm (3 in) in diameter. Each rosette is home to one pinkish-coloured larva of a gall midge, *Rhabdophaga rosaria*.

Horsechestnut

There are two birds with willow added to their names, willow tit and willow warbler. Willow is one of the willow tit's favourite nesting places, particularly if the willows are in damp woodland where there are usually mossy tree stumps decaying among the undergrowth.

Here the tits excavate a nest hole, being very careful to carry any debris well away from the site so that no tell-tale traces of their building are left close to the nest. Willow tits do use birch and elder trees too. Marsh and willow tits are very much alike in appearance, but marsh tits build their nests lined with moss and feathers in a natural hole or crevice. Both birds feed their young on caterpillars, aphids, flies, small beetles and spiders; if you are lucky enough to be able to watch the activities of parent birds, you will probably find that they return to the nest with food about 20 times an hour.

Willow warblers are well-camouflaged birds; they are greeny-brown above and creamy-buff below, and they merge into the background in a shy way. Their ideal habitats range from damp woodlands – where willows grow, as their name suggests – to conifer plantations; here the female constructs a beautiful nest of grass stems, bracken, moss and lichen, lined with down and hidden among low-growing plants and bushes. Warblers have fine, narrow bills, perfect for picking up and catching tiny insects and caterpillars.

HAZEL

Hazel, *Corylus avellana*, will grow into a small tree. It is found in most well-established hedgerows, where the pollen-laden lamb's tail catkins are cheerful signs of spring early in the year. If you look at the hazel in autumn you will see the male catkins already waiting for spring, tightly closed but very easily seen. The female flowers have to be searched for; they are fat buds with red, tassel-like stigmas sticking out, like plumes from a helmet. The sticky stigmas wave in the breeze, catching pollen that comes drifting by.

A hazel leaf in autumn

Hazel is also a common undershrub of oak woodland. In the past, stands of hazel were coppiced every seven years or so and the resulting poles were made into portable fencing called hurdles; these were panels of pliable, split hazel poles woven together into what was known as wattle work. Hazel wattle work was also used to make the walls of medieval timber-framed houses; the wattle was daubed with plaster, hence the term 'wattle and daub'. Early man used a wattle frame for the coracle boats needed for fishing or fording rivers. Hazel poles were used in thatching and as bean poles and clothes props, and made into lobster pots and salmon traps.

Occasionally you may see a hawthorn and hazel hedge that has been laid; this is an old craft that used to be carried out during the winter months. Beginning at the far left of the hedge, the shrubs are trimmed of their side branches leaving the main stems, which are cut halfway through near the base and then carefully bent over at a low angle. Each stem is laid over to the left, so clearing the way for the next cut; the end result is a neat row of bent-over stems, often 3 metres (10 ft) long and all overlapping. Every metre (3 ft) or so, a stake of ash or chestnut is driven into the ground through the angled stems, forming a rough weave. This all results in a good strong windbreak which gives shelter to cattle in wet weather and keeps them safely in the field.

There are about 70 insects associated with hazel, including more than 30 large moths. It is probably a good thing that none of these have larvae which eat hazel exclusively, as some of them are excellent defoliators, notably the mottled umber and buff-tip.

Mottled umber are red-brown looper caterpillars who, when disturbed, drop from the leaves and hang suspended on a silken thread until any danger has passed. Buff-tip larvae are gregarious; large groups of these yellow-gold and black caterpillars strip the foliage from trees, branch by branch, in a very methodical way.

Some caterpillars are distinctive, while others are well camouflaged. Lobster moth larvae are reddy-brown with fin-like flanges at the rear, pointed humps on segments four to eight, and strongly developed front legs; the adult moths are sombre grey. The adults of the large emerald moth are very beautiful, green, feathery insects, yet the caterpillars camouflage themselves to look like twigs.

Many birds feed their young on caterpillars and other juicy invertebrates, not only for the protein but also for the water content, which is important to the fledglings.

Aphids and capsid bugs attack many leaves, including hazel; these leaf bugs are eaten by birds, ladybirds and their larvae, lace-wings and their larvae, and the larvae of some hover flies. Look for the black-kneed capsid, a green insect with black 'knee' joints; it is mainly predatory, feeding on red spider mites.

Nut weevils – weevils are the beetles with 'noses' – attack hazel nuts. The females lay eggs in the developing fruits; the larvae eat the kernels, and when they are fully grown they bore their way out through the shell and drop to the ground to pupate. A small hole in the nut shell indicates that a weevil has been in residence.

Dormice eat insects, beech-mast, acorns and fruits of all kinds, including haws and hazelnuts. Common, or hazel, dormice like to live in hazel thickets where the cover and the food are good. Here they climb around with great ease; they are usually nocturnal, so they have

Short & long food chains

Short chains give more energy to the top predator. This is important when food is scarce.

aphid

↑

ladybird

↑

leaf

There is only one generation of ladybirds a year but the 100 or so larvae eat around 130,000 aphids in their lifetime. The adults also eat aphids.

badger

↑

shrew

↑

beetle

↑

weevil larva in pupation

↑

developing fruit

Long chains give less energy to the top predator.

large eyes and long tactile whiskers to help them in the dark. But one afternoon I saw a mother dormouse moving her babies, one by one, to a safer nesting site. Dormice get their name from the six month dormancy period which enables them to avoid hard seasons. Hibernation is usually spent at, or just below, ground level in a snug nest. I once found a hibernating dormouse in a manure heap; its knees were tucked up to its middle, its front paws were tucked under its chin and its furry tail was wrapped part way round its head, like a scarf.

The summer nest made by a dormouse is oval; it may be made of grass, but often it is woven from strips of honeysuckle bark. Honeysuckle is a plant of mixed deciduous woodland and hedgerows, where it twines its clockwise way so tightly that it can make barley sugar twists of the stems of young trees. You may have seen walking sticks made from stems that have been twisted in this way. Honeysuckle flowers open in early summer, and their main pollinators are hawkmoths and bumble bees. Early grey moths and gold spangle moths put their eggs on honeysuckle leaves, as do the clearwing and the broad-bordered bee hawkmoths and white admiral butterflies.

Among the hedgerow plants you will find several members of the parsley family, the umbellifers, with their umbrellas of flowers. Many insects visit the flowers, which glisten with nectar. The insects along a hedgerow attract birds, shrews and hedgehogs. The birds are preyed upon by kestrels and sparrowhawks; owls hunt for shrews, voles, woodmice and dormice and the stealthy fox doesn't bat a whisker at the prickles on a hedgehog.

Sloes, fruits of the blackthorn

BLACKTHORN AND BRAMBLE

Blackthorn, *Prunus spinosa*, and bramble, *Rubus fruticosus*, are both in the same family as the hawthorn, Rosaceae; so insects in association with hawthorn also use these plants. Blackthorn and bramble are both thicket-forming, offering good nesting sites to robins, wrens, dunnocks, linnets, yellowhammers and visiting nightingales.

Blackthorn spreads along the hedge line by sending up shoots a metre or more (3–4 ft) away from the main stem. Left alone, these shoots will grow and multiply and form a thicket that is so thorny that it is a very safe refuge.

Brown hairstreak butterflies, old lady moths and the gregarious, web-forming brown tail caterpillars are

Honeysuckle berries

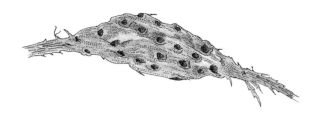

among the many insects who favour the blackthorn. Brown hairstreaks overwinter in the egg stage attached to twigs; this makes them very vulnerable to food-hunting birds.

Brambles claw their way to the light by using their merciless, sharp thorns. Brambles colonize and are colonized; the plant is a fortified refuge with a built-in food supply.

Bramble stems are used by a tiny gall wasp, *Diastrophus rubi*, who lays many eggs under the epidermis. When the eggs hatch, the wriggling larvae cause the plant tissues to swell, forming a gall which provides the larvae with food. Each larva eats out a tiny chamber for itself, until the whole gall becomes like a block of flats. Used galls have holes showing where the uninvited guests have been.

Bramble leaves are eaten in early spring by deer, rabbits and hares; goats will eat them all the year round. Emperor moth caterpillars use bramble leaves as one of their food supplies; they can also be found on blackthorn, heather and sallow.

You have probably seen the white trails of leaf miners on bramble leaves. Leaf miners are the larvae of very small moths or sawflies. Tiny eggs are laid singly on the leaves, and the minute larva bites its way into the palisade tissue of the leaf, between the upper and lower epidermis; there it eats plant cells.

Some larvae make a serpentine 'mine' that widens as the larva grows; others make a blotch mine by eating the surrounding tissue. You may see trail mines on honeysuckle leaves and blotch mines on holly leaves, because different species choose different leaves.

Spiders spin their webs among the bramble's thorny stems and lie in wait for insect prey; they may themselves be eaten by birds – especially wrens.

Many insects visit bramble flowers. White admiral butterflies are seen in summer and hoverflies enjoy the nectar, as do many bees. The fruits are eaten by many animals, including butterflies such as ringlet, comma, speckled wood and red admiral; wasps sit on the fruits enjoying the juicy delights and deeply resenting any disturbance, as blackberry pickers find to their cost. Birds, foxes, badgers, squirrels, hedgehogs, voles, wood mice and dormice also eat the fruits. Many blackberry seeds are sown in piles of dung, when they pass through a gut undigested; these seeds grow in an area often well away from the parent plant, so starting a new bramble patch. By early autumn the fruits are softened by frosts and tainted by mildew, making it easy for flesh flies, bluebottles and greenbottles to dribble their saliva on to the fruit and suck up the juices released by the enzymes.

Bramble stem galled by the tiny gall wasp Diastrophus rubi. *The hover fly,* Syrphus ribesii *(below), is one of the insects that visit bramble flowers.*

Greenbottle, Lucilia caesar, *and a red admiral butterfly enjoy the soft and succulent blackberries.*

108

Shade-loving plants will grow around the roots of the thicket-forming plants. Ivy is a very useful plant to animals who nest among its branches, hibernate in its protection, hide from predators and hunt for food. Ivy is the last plant to flower in the year, and is pollinated by wasps and flies. The berries are eaten by birds, who are glad of food in the depths of winter.

The holly blue butterfly often uses ivy as a food plant. The first holly blues emerge in the middle of spring, and within a few weeks they lay their eggs in developing holly flowers. The caterpillars soon hatch and eat the holly flowers and any of their kin they encounter. The full, fat caterpillars pupate in the middle of summer, hanging from holly leaves. The second batch of adults are on the wing a month later and, as there aren't any holly flowers to lay eggs in, the butterflies choose ivy buds as food for their young. The caterpillars pupate in the ivy through the winter.

The leaves on the flowering stems of ivy do not have lobes.

IN THE SHADOW OF THE HEDGEROW

The grasses growing along a hedgerow are food for many caterpillars. Cock's foot is the larval food of the gatekeeper, speckled wood and wall butterflies and of the lesser yellow underwing moth. Couch grass feeds drinker, dark arches and flounced rustic moth caterpillars. Meadow brown and ringlet butterflies put their eggs on annual meadow grass, while skippers use Yorkshire fog, sheep's fescue and false brome. Cat's tail grass is food for the well camouflaged caterpillars of marbled white butterflies.

Nettles grow where there has been a disturbance in the soil. About 30 species of insects rely on the nettle for food, and more than 100 include it in their diet.

Slugs and snails creep about the plants along the hedgerow. Hedgehogs, thrushes and pigeons look-out for them, and snails also fall prey to glow worm larvae.

Glow worms are beetles, and the male is very beetle-like, with hard wing covers protecting gauzy wings. The female is larger; she is larva-like and wingless. It is the female who has more 'glow'; a yellow-green luminous light shines from the last three abdominal segments when she 'switches on'. It is a cold light, so no energy is wasted in heat. The light is produced by the breakdown of a substance called luciferin, which glows in the presence of oxygen and water, with help from active enzymes. Below the self-renewing layer of luciferin there is a strip of opaque

Some of the butterflies and moths who
lay their eggs on nettle leaves.
From the top reading clockwise:
red admiral hovering and a comma
flying in
European map butterflies
plain golden Y moth
red admiral
peacock (in centre)
scarlet tiger moth
dark spectacle
painted lady
small tortoiseshell
comma
beautiful golden Y moth

crystals which act as reflectors and prevent the light from being reabsorbed into the glow worm's body. The female glow worm sits in a bush or amongst the grasses and switches on her light to attract a male. He flies along with his two little pinpoints of light shining, looking round with his wonderful, many-faceted eyes. Suddenly the lights go out – they've found each other!

Glow worm larvae are small and dark grey; they hunt for snails. The larva seizes its prey in curved mandibles, injects a digestive fluid into it and waits for the snail to turn into a soup, conveniently dished up in its own shell. It takes about three years for the larva to grow to pupation stage.

Glow worms are getting scarce. The spraying of herbicides and insecticides doesn't help, and the female glow worm faces competition from street lights. The males think that they have found a wonderful female and dash themselves to death on the hot glass.

Violets and primroses grow on shady hedgebanks: these are pollinated by long-tongued bees and bee flies.

So it goes on; each section of the hedge has its visitors and predators, its food chains and its food webs. We may take these secret lives for granted, but their stories really are interesting.

Overleaf. *A chart of the trees, shrubs, climbing and scrambling plants you may find in a hedgerow near you.*

Pussy willow

The hawthorn has white flowers in late spring followed by red fruits called haws.

Sallow, or pussy willow, has silky, silver grey catkins in early to mid spring.

Hazel has long male catkins. The female flowers are short red tufts. You can find them in late winter.

 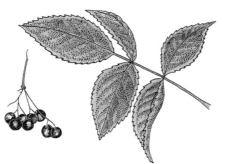 

Ash trees have black leaf buds. Flowers without sepals or petals open in the middle of spring.

Elder has creamy white flowers in early to mid summer, followed by black fruits.

Spindle fruits are rosy pink; these split to show fleshy orange-yellow seed covers.

Dog roses bloom in early to mid summer. The red fruits are called rose hips.

Hop stems twine clockwise. The female flowers hang in groups of cone-like bracts.

Ivy is an evergreen climbing plant. The yellow-green flowers open in mid autumn.

  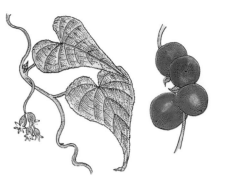

Wild clematis is also called traveller's joy or old man's beard.

White bryony scrambles and clings by means of tightly wrapping tendrils.

Black bryony twines in an anti-clockwise direction.

Holly trees are prickly evergreens. The white flowers bloom in late spring.

Blackthorn, or sloe flowers in early to mid-spring before the leaves unfurl.

Field maples are related to sycamores. The flowers are greenish-yellow in late spring.

Common blackthorn has round black berries and sharp thorny twigs.

Alder buckthorn does not have thorns. The berries are red and purple.

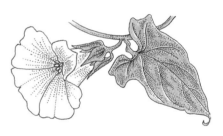

Guelder rose has fragrant flowers in late spring and early summer; these are followed by red berries.

Blackberry stems sprawl or scramble, creating a thorny tangled mass.

Honeysuckle stems climb clockwise. The leaves are in opposite pairs.

Hedge bindweed stems twine in an anti-clockwise direction.

Cleavers, or sweethearts, has many tiny prickles which make its surfaces adhesive.

Woody nightshade threads its stems among other plants to gain support.

Bush vetch has trailing tendrils which reach out to cling to other plants.

Woodland World

Before we came to live in Derbyshire we had an old house in East Sussex, with ⅓ hectare (1 acre) of mixed woodland. I can't tell you how much pleasure that little piece of woodland gave me – no matter what the season. Woods and copses have a life-style of their very own, and the intricate relationships within the woodland ecosystem would give a lifetime of study to anyone.

To walk into a wood very early on a morning in late spring is my idea of heaven. To listen for the cascading song of warblers, the bell-like chime of tits and the clear songs of black-caps and white-throats. To smell the wood garlic and feast my eyes on bugle, bluebells, wood anemone, greater stitchwort, violets and primroses. To hear the buzz of insects making merry, and to feel the protection of the old tree trunks rising up all around, throwing their branches wide and spreading their unfurling leaves to the warming sun.

Trees are wonderful plants, so long in the living and the growing and the being there for so many animals to live on, and in, and around. They are home for mosses and lichens that grow in amongst the flaking bark; for fungi that sprout among the roots, and for ferns that spring from ancient branches. Animals make or find holes in the craggy trunk, and nests may be tucked comfortably into the crook of a branch.

Sit among the roots of a tree, with your back against the trunk, and feel at one with it. The longer you sit quietly there, the more you will see and hear, and the more you will feel at peace with your soul. Lie on your back and look at the leaf canopy: each leaf is part of a mosaic pattern, catching as much light as possible.

WOODLANDS

We can learn about the history of our vegetation by making an analysis of the pollen found in peat and sediments. Pollen grains of particular plants can be identified because they have a characteristic pattern of ridges, pores and other markings. When airborne pollen settles on a water surface, it usually sinks down through the water and into the sediment below. Similarly, when pollen lands on peaty ground, it becomes embedded in a peat layer. Under both these circumstances, the pollen grains remain intact and preserved in a particular layer – above last year's layer and below next year's.

By boring into the sediment, or the peat, and taking out core samples, scientists can examine the pollen deposits of thousands of years, all in chronological order. The dates of the layers can be estimated accurately by a process called carbon dating. When samples from different deposited layers are examined, and the pollen types and relative numbers of grains present are recorded, a picture emerges of the major changes in vegetation over a long period of time.

Particular plants favour particular climatic conditions, so pollen analysis means major climatic changes can be recognized too.

If you have a microscope, you may find it interesting to collect pollen from various plants and have a look at the patterns and grooves on the exine – the outer skin. Compare the smooth pollen grains of wind-pollinated plants, such as hazel and wood anemone, with the spiky pollen of insect-pollinated plants, such as primroses and greater stitchwort. Wind-pollinated plants produce copious amounts of pollen because so much of it is likely to miss the mark. The pollen is light and has a smooth exine to lower its resistance to the wind. The spiky or patterned pollen of insect-pollinated plants is better able to cling to the hairs of pollinating insects.

About 10,000 years ago, at the end of the last Ice Age, most of Britain and northern Europe was tundra, frozen for much of the year but supporting low-growing plants such as lichen, mosses, bilberry and juniper.

At this time Britain was still joined to the continent of Europe so, as the ice sheet gradually retreated northwards and the summers became warmer and the winters less severe, plant life began to spread from the southern parts of Europe which had not been ice bound.

The first real trees to grow were very hardy: birch, rowan, hazel, willow and Scots pine. As the climate improved, the pine-dominated woodlands spread

*Meadow brown
butterfly*

Opposite. *Tree stools in a coppice woodland have been known to live for hundreds of years.*

Harebell

115

northwards. The animals associated with these woodlands moved northwards too, probably including red squirrels, red deer, wild boar and wolves.

The climate continued to improve, enabling elm, alder, oak, beech and small-leaved lime trees to replace the Scots pine. The pines were gradually driven further and further north to the Scottish Highlands, where their descendants grow today in conditions too harsh for other trees to compete.

The land mass of Europe separated from Britain about 7,000 years ago. This prevented animals migrating to and from Britain, with the exception of the more mobile species such as birds.

In about 8,000 BC the world population probably did not exceed five million people. As a hunter gatherer, nomadic man did not have many possessions; the women in such societies could not undertake food-gathering expeditions with more than one infant. So births were probably spaced out to about one every four years, keeping the population fairly constant. When the nomadic way of life changed to a more settled one, the restriction on births was lifted and population figures began to rise.

Within a community, the change from gathering wild wheat grains to growing plants of it would be easy and natural. You can imagine how some of the grains may have been spilt accidentally and, when wheat grew in that particular place the following year, the spillage would be remembered and the accident turned into a lesson in husbandry. In this way the hunter gatherers became farmers.

When agricultural man moved into a new area, he chopped down the trees or ring-barked them to destroy their growth. The area cleared by tree-cutting was used for farming until the minerals in the soil were used up; then the area was left to regenerate and the farmers moved on to clear more land. All this time the population was growing, and people were living longer because they were better fed. Overcrowding had begun, and with it came a great demand for wood.

During the Middle Ages that demand increased as towns were built and crafts and industries developed. Wood was needed for building, for fires and to make tools; mining, glassworks and iron foundries all needed wood as fuel. Gradually, the wooded areas around industrial towns literally disappeared in smoke; while in warmer agricultural areas woodlands had been destroyed to provide fields and pasture. By the end of the eighteenth century, there was a great deal of anxiety about the fate of the disappearing forests – more, I would

Sweet chestnuts are encased in a prickly husk.

Elderberries are rich in vitamin C.

Hop fruits flavour beer.

say, from the point of view of a lack of resources for industry than for the sake of the woodlands themselves. Reforestation of empty spaces began in the early nineteenth century; spruces and pines were the favourite trees to plant as they grow so quickly. In this way man, with good intentions but not enough knowledge, altered the structure of European forests and upset the delicate balance of nature.

Population increases come in surges; the industrial age brought a massive increase in the numbers of people, while the recent medical revolution has produced healthier, longer-lived people. Populations cannot go on increasing at the present rate. The surface of the earth is limited, and so are its resources. Humanity threatens not only its own survival but that of the Earth itself.

DECIDUOUS WOODLAND

Most woodland areas have one or two species of trees that outnumber the others. The tree that is present in the largest numbers is called the dominant species. These dominant trees influence all other plant life in the wood, and the plant life in its turn influences the animal life. If there are two species in more or less equal numbers, they are 'co-dominant'.

There are several types of woodland, depending on the local soil and climate. These include damp oak-wood, dry oak-wood, ash-wood, beech-wood, birch-wood, alder carr and plantations of mixed woodland.

The most common woodland type in Britain is dominated by oak. Throughout the last few centuries the number of oak-woods has been greatly influenced by the economy. Oak timber was highly valued for house- and ship-building; many oak trees were planted and the woodlands were managed for timber and for the oak bark, which provided tannic acid for the growing tanning industry.

There are two species of native British oak, both found throughout the country. The common or pedunculate oak, *Quercus robur*, prefers the heavy clay soils of the lowlands; while the durmast or sessile oak, *Quercus petraea*, favours the shallow, lighter soil of the uplands.

Oak trees have both male and female flowers, which open in late spring just after the leaves have expanded. Pedunculate oak has very short-stemmed leaves which have ear-like (auriculate) lobes at the base and are quite smooth in texture underneath. The twigs are rugged and the oval leaf buds are spirally arranged, with a cluster of

'Large oaks from little acorns grow.'

QUERCUS ROBUR, pedunculate oak. This oak has very short-stemmed leaves with ear-like lobes at the base.

117

buds at the tip. The female flowers on their long stalks are carried near the tips of the twigs, and the male catkins hang further back. The acorns of this oak are carried on long stalks; these are the peduncles which give the species its common name.

Sessile means stalkless, and the acorns of *Quercus petraea* are borne on very, very short stalks. The female flowers are carried in the leaf axils near the tips of the twigs, and the male flowers hang further back, in a similar way to those of the pedunculate oak. The leaves of the sessile oak have long stalks and the leaf base is tapered, lacking the auricles of the pedunculate oak. The leaves are downy beneath.

Oak trees endure fungal diseases and insect plagues without lasting harm; they are very long-lived plants.

Most woodlands have four distinct layers of vegetation:

1. The tree or canopy layer. This is composed of the leaves and branches of the dominant or co-dominant species. Any vegetation beneath these dominant trees will receive only as much light as can filter through from above. Beech trees cast such a deep shade that few plants can live in their shadow.
2. The shrub layer. This consists of small tree species such as hazel, hawthorn, holly, dog rose and bramble, depending on the soil conditions in the area.
3. The field, or herb, layer. The plants in this layer are non-woody. They live beneath the tree and shrub layers, and receive only a low light intensity. In compensation they are well shielded from winds, their surrounding temperature is more equable and the humidity in the air is higher than for plants in the upper layers.

   Nevertheless, it is difficult for seedlings to become established in these shady situations, so the plants in this layer are usually perennial – living for three years or more. These herbaceous plants produce leaves early in the year before the canopy closes over to restrict the light. Many have an early spurt of growth and flowering and are less active or die back in summer. Some woodland plant species have specialized food-storage organs: for example the bulbs of bluebell and allium, the corms of sow bread (wild cyclamen), the tubers of lesser celandine and the rhizomes of wood anemones. Others spread by runners – look at the way a bramble colonizes a piece of ground.
4. The ground layer is the lowest layer of all. Here you will find plants which are evergreen throughout the year: algae, liverwort, lichen and mosses.

Acorns of the pedunculate oak are carried on long stalks. These are the peduncles which give the tree its name.

QUERCUS PETRAEA, SESSILE OAK. This oak has long-stalked leaves with a tapered or rounded base.

Acorns of the sessile oak are borne on very short stems. Sessile means stalkless & the tree takes its name from this feature.

Look carefully at your local wood. Can you see its layers? Notice at what time of the year the trees flower. It always surprises me to find how many people do not realize that woodland trees do flower; where the fruits are to come from if they don't is a mystery!

Each woodland layer has its own animal community. Each plant species in that layer has its own particular association of insects, and these provide a food source for insect-eating birds.

Many birds nest in one woodland layer and feed in another; most stay in the wood for both food and shelter. For example:

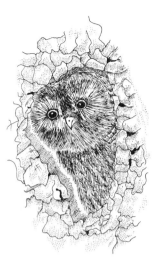

The tawny owl likes to nest in a hole in a tree.

CANOPY LAYER:	FEEDING	— willow warbler, nuthatch, bluetit
	NESTING	— goldcrest, woodpigeon, carrion crow, heron
SHRUB LAYER:	FEEDING	— great tit, wren, goldcrest
	NESTING	— blackbird, song thrush, wren
FIELD LAYER:	FEEDING	— woodpigeon, blackbird, pheasant
	NESTING	— willow warbler, pheasant, nightingale

Some birds, such as herons and carrion crows, nest in the canopy layer and feed outside the wood.

The competition for food is very fierce, particularly between members of the same species; so, before the breeding season, many birds stake out a territory and defend it strongly. The territory includes the nest and the feeding ground around it. Song birds proclaim their territory by perching on a song post and singing a distinctive song. The holding of territories ensures that birds are spread out, so sharing out the available food.

Woods are full of hidden life, much of which is active only at dawn, at dusk and after dark; so when you walk through a wood you will be lucky if you see any animals. They will have heard you coming, and may even lurk in a safe place to watch you walk by. Sometimes shrews can be seen scampering along their runs; I think they become so engrossed in shrill arguments with their neighbours that they ignore humans. I once discovered a shrew highroad, where a shrew corridor ran through the grass in a wood; there I was able to watch a mother shrew with a line of babies behind her, each one holding on to the tail of the one in front, like a daisy chain; shrews were hunting and shrews were going back home to rest. The noise was surprising; whenever a shrew encountered another, the little bodies reverberated with their squeals and squeaks and they made no attempt to keep quiet.

Their method of feeding is quite unlike that of other tiny mammals; instead of the front feet being used to

The nuthatch searches for spiders & insects in cracks in the tree bark, searching in the crevices as it comes down the tree head first.

carry food to the mouth, they are used to hold the food down and stop it wriggling while it is being eaten. Shrews and moles, which are also found in woods, eat earthworms, insect larvae and slugs. Shrews also eat beetles, spiders, flies and woodlice.

Wood mice are nocturnal burrowers with underground runways leading to a nest of grass below, or sometimes above, ground.

Yellow-necked mice are more active than wood mice; they are slightly larger and are extremely good climbers. A yellow-necked mouse climbed up the gable end of our house last summer, to escape from a cat; it hung on to the wall for about 20 minutes before turning round and coming down again. It was probably a yellow-necked mouse that ran up the clock, in the nursery rhyme! They certainly climb trees in a wood, where they nibble buds and shoots.

Both species of mice eat cereals, soft fruits and their seeds, nuts, fungi, plant galls and overwintering larvae found in the soil. The mice produce many young; their life expectancy is short for they have many predators.

Voles are common in deciduous woodland. They may be heard during the day, twittering and chattering as they scamper along their shallow runways. Voles and the mice found in woods are hunted by owls, stoats, weasels, foxes and badgers.

In winter it is often possible to spot squirrels' dreys in the canopy layer. You may see other evidence of squirrels in the wood; look for places where the bark has been stripped from trees. When I planted the trees in my wild garden, I was careful to fit a plastic tree guard around each one, as a protection from rabbits and squirrels. Grey squirrels are bold and inquisitive; they are able to leap as much as 4 metres (1 ft) from tree to tree and to race up vertical trunks.

Invertebrates are a very important part of life in a woodland. They are food for several small mammals and for birds; most seed-eating birds feed their nestlings on insects until the young birds can manage harder food and are able to fly to water to drink.

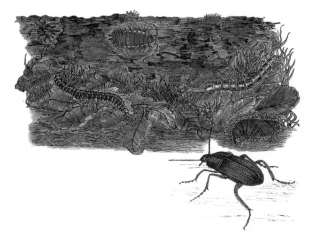

Here are a woodlouse, a centipede, a millipede and a ground beetle around a dead log. An earthworm and the pupa of a pale tussock moth are just below the soil surface.

Rowan berries

120

Lime fruits hang from a green leaf-like bract.

THERE'S LIFE IN DEAD WOOD

A log in a moist part of a shady wood is a good place to watch invertebrate life. But you must be patient and wait for things to happen naturally, because if you break open the dead wood to speed things up, you will destroy the habitat you are looking at.

Moss often grows on the bark of trees. Look at some through a magnifying glass: it looks like a miniature jungle through which moss snails roam, and red soil mites and pseudoscorpions hunt. Look at the cracks in loose bark; mesh web spiders may be in residence, with a tangled surface web designed to catch crawling insects. Or you may find gallery patterns, a sign that bark beetles have moved in.

Bark beetles are often the first occupants of a dead tree. The adult beetles gnaw through the outer bark and tunnel a little gallery where they mate. The female elongates the pairing gallery, gnawing tiny niches at intervals along its walls and putting an egg into each niche. When the eggs hatch, each larva gnaws at its own gallery, extending outwards and more or less at right angles to the main one. As the larvae grow, the galleries increase in width to accommodate their little fat bodies, until they finally end in pupal cells. The beetles that emerge gnaw a short tunnel out of the bark and you may find exit holes where the beetles have left.

These activities loosen the bark of the tree, making it possible for other creatures to get in. Woodlice enjoy this habitat; they eat decaying vegetation, fungi and wood, and they need to live in damp conditions as their body covering is not waterproof and they dry out in open, sunny places. Female woodlice do not lay their eggs and leave them hidden; instead they keep them in pockets underneath their body, where the young hatch. If you look at a woodlouse through a magnifying glass in spring, you may see the tiny white babies hanging on to their mother. You will see then why woodlice are called sowbugs in some parts of the country; the babies really do look like little piglets lying in a row.

The larvae of wood boring beetles tunnel into wood; many hover fly larvae can also be found in partly decayed wood. Remember that all the invertebrates living in and round a habitat are a source of food for other animals.

A moss snail shell (left), is only 6 mm (¼ in) long. Pseudoscorpions and red soil mites are in the spider family.

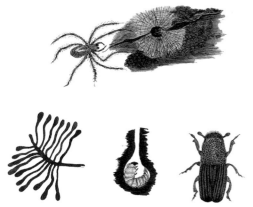

Mesh web spiders are 11 mm (nearly ½ in) long.

Elm bark beetles make tunnels beneath the bark; their larvae make individual tunnels.

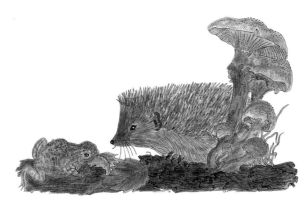

Toads and hedgehogs hunt among the logs; honey fungus attacks living and dead wood.

HERMAPHRODITE GASTROPODS
Slugs and Snails

Slugs and snails are gastropods, which means 'stomach foot'. The animals have a fleshy foot, which secretes a silvery mucus on which they glide along. They feed at night and after daytime rain, when the air is damp and there is little chance of their drying out.

In hot weather snails aestivate in a sheltered place, pulling themselves into their shells and plugging up the opening with layers of mucus, which hardens. In winter they hibernate in the same way.

Slugs do not have an external shell to protect them, but many have a saddle-shaped plate under the outer skin behind the head. They have a thick coat of protective slime and an ability to move quickly; they can also contract their bodies into crevices to escape predators.

Slugs and snails are hermaphrodites, which means that every individual has both male and female sex organs. Each one can mate with any other of its species, and all are able to lay eggs.

The mating of snails is a lengthy affair, preceded by a courtship ritual during which the partners circle one another, caressing each other with their sensitive touch tentacles. Then they rise, pressing their bodies together. At the peak of this courtship, each snail fires a harpoon-like calcareous dart into the body of its partner; this sharp dig in the side is the trigger for sperm exchange.

If you are able to find banded snails in shady places in your area, collect some from different habitats and see how much they vary in colour. Each form is usually more frequent in the habitat in which it is best camouflaged. Snails found against the broken background of a mixed hedgerow usually have quite distinct bands, snails found against the more uniform background of beech leaf litter are usually unbanded, while those found in grass are mainly yellow and those living against the dark background of bark or dead leaves are mainly brown or pink. There are intermediate conditions favouring snails with varying numbers of bands, where different forms may be found in more or less even numbers.

The condition of the habitat changes through the year, and the snail communities have to change their background if they are to stay camouflaged from predators.

Great grey slugs often perform a rope trick during their courtship and mating. The two slugs climb a wall or a tree trunk and one produces a thick rope of mucus from which the slugs hang suspended, slowly swaying as they

Slugs are able to contract their bodies into small spaces.

Snails have shells which protect them from extreme weather conditions & from some predators.

The mating of snails.

Great grey slugs often perform a rope trick during their courtship & mating.

122

encircle each other before exchanging sperm. Then they separate; the first slug to leave climbs the rope, while the second either eats its way up the mucus strand, or falls to the ground. I have seen this performance take place in an open doorway and from a fence crossbar.

Flowers of the oak tree

Fruits of the London plane

Ash keys hang on the tree right through the winter.

COPPICE WOODLAND

You may have seen a wood that has been coppiced and wondered why it had been treated so. Coppicing is a way of managing a broad-leaved woodland in order to provide a continual supply of various sizes of wood.

A coppiced woodland is divided into several areas. Each area is cut in turn on a cycle of seven to ten years or more. The trees are cut down to ground level, leaving a 'stool' from which new straight shoots will grow. Rising above the coppiced wood there may be some 'standard' trees, left to grow to their prime – 70 to 150 years.

The coppice-with-standards method of woodland management dates back to ancient times; it is a traditional method which benefits woodland wildlife. Each area of the wood, from the part that is newly cut to the patch that has grown again and casts a deep shade, encourages a different set of animal species adapted to a different set of conditions.

Butterflies, birds and other animals do not have far to move to find their ideal habitat. Seeds shed in a newly cut area are able to germinate and grow successfully in the light conditions. A year after the cut, the field layer is at its best and is visited by many insects. Five years or so later, new shoots have grown from the stools to create a dense thicket where birds such as blackcaps, yellow-hammers, nightingales and whitethroats like to nest.

If you find a coppice to explore, look at the tree stools; animals often use them as look-out posts or feeding stations. You will probably find evidence to support this.

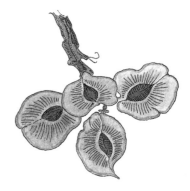

Wych elm fruits have wings to carry them away from the parent tree.

FLOWERLESS PLANTS

Algae grow in the rain tracks on tree trunks and on the wet bases; lichens, liverworts and mosses also grow on tree trunks and in shady, moist places; the damp, rich woodland floors provide favourable conditions for the growth of ferns.

Woodland areas of all types provide many places where flowerless plants are able to grow in the damp atmosphere created by the trees. Flowerless or spore-producing plants evolved more than 500 million years ago, so they are far older than plants which have flowers and produce seeds. Seeds are complex structures made of many cells: each seed contains an embryo plant and a food store contained in a protective seed coat. Spores are comparatively simple: each is a single cell with a very limited food reserve and a thin cell wall which offers little protection. New plants develop from spores in a rather complicated way which I will try to explain.

FERNS

Ferns have two distinct and alternating stages in their life-cycle: the prothallus, which is short-lived, and the fern plant itself.

The leaf of a fern is called a frond. When the frond is very young it is coiled tightly and is called a crozier, because it looks like the staff or crook of a bishop.

During the summer, spore cases containing many spores grow in clusters on the underside of the fern frond. Usually the spore cases ripen at different times, making sure that the spores are shed over a period of time. When the spores fall on to wet ground, they grow into tiny heart-shaped structures called prothalli – measuring about 5 mm (⅕ in) across.

Each prothallus contains male and female reproductive cells. In the wet conditions, male cells – sperm – swim through the film of water to the female receptacle; this is equivalent to pollination in the flowering plant. Fertilization takes place when the sperm fuses with the egg cell in the receptacle.

A new fern plant grows from the receptacle and depends on the prothallus for food until its own roots and fronds begin to grow.

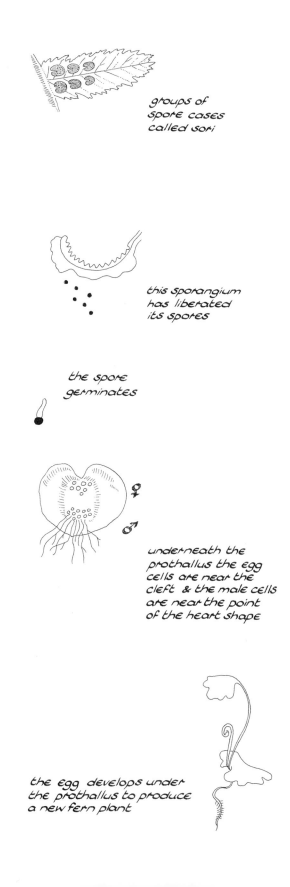

groups of spore cases called sori

this sporangium has liberated its spores

the spore germinates

♀
♂

underneath the prothallus the egg cells are near the cleft & the male cells are near the point of the heart shape

the egg develops under the prothallus to produce a new fern plant

MOSSES

Mosses have alternating stages, too. Their structure is very simple. They have stems and leaves but no real roots; instead they have root-like structures – rhizoids.

Mosses reproduce by spores which develop in stalked capsules. You must have seen these little orange capsules growing from moss in all sorts of places – walls, paths, fences, tree trunks and branches. When the sun catches them they look very pretty. When the spores inside the capsules are ripe they are released through small openings, like pepper from a pepper pot.

On the ground the spores develop into new moss plants. In most species, each tiny plant contains male and female structures, though in some these male and female structures are on separate plants.

During wet weather, the female cells secrete a chemical which guides the male's sperm to them through a film of water on the plant. Once fertilized, the female develops a capsule which in turn produces spores.

Moss reproduction

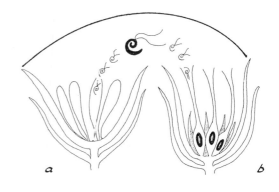

This is a greatly enlarged diagram of male & female moss plants. a. shows the antherozoids (sperm) swimming through a dew drop or rain drop to b. the female. The antherozoids swim down the neck of the structures which carry the egg cells at their base.

FUNGI

Many fungi live in woodland conditions. They do not have the green pigment chlorophyll, and so are unable to manufacture their own carbohydrates in the way green plants do. So they must obtain their food in other ways: some live on dead wood; some feed as parasites on living trees; others live in the ground and have a close and friendly relationship – symbiosis – with particular trees which vary from species to species. The fungus *Boletus elegans* is found in association with larch, and *Amanita muscaria* – fly agaric – favours birch trees.

The fungi which live on the dead remains of former living things such as rotting wood, leaf mould, old bread and cheese are called saprophytes. These fungi, together with bacteria, are important in the decay and decomposition of dead remains and waste products. They help to produce basic raw materials for the nutrition of green plants. Yeast has been used for thousands of years in baking and brewing. It is a saprophytic fungus that lives on sugars; it also grows naturally on the skin of fruit.

Parasitic fungi harm and may kill the host with which they associate. They include the brown rot of apples and the rusts and smuts which attack crops.

The actively growing and feeding parts of a fungus are called hyphae; these are fine branching threads which spread over and penetrate the food material. The hyphae

Fungi

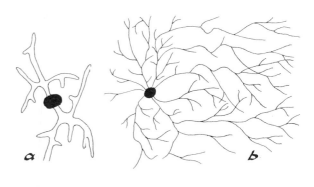

a: germination of a spore, magnified.
b: spore in the centre of a mycelium of hyphal threads.

ground level

A mushroom is formed from a compacted mass of hyphae which enlarges as water is taken up.

then pour out digestive enzymes which reduce carbohydrates and other complex compounds to more simple soluble forms which the hyphae can absorb.

The hyphae of the symbiotic fungi penetrate some of the tree's roots and form a dense covering over the surface. Each chosen root becomes thick and fleshy under its covering of fungal hyphae, and is called a mycorrhiza. Water and mineral salts absorbed from the soil by the fungus are quickly made available to the roots, while the fungus takes food materials such as sugars from the roots for its own benefit. These fungi are particularly important during the early life of a tree as they help it to grow well in the midst of a great deal of competition.

The mushrooms, toadstools, puff-balls and bracket fungi we find in a wood are the fruiting bodies which carry millions of spores. Under favourable conditions, some of the hyphae just below the soil or the tree part mass together to form a globular shape that pushes its way into the open. As this mass of hyphae grows, it becomes the shape of the fungus we recognize: a field mushroom, an earthstar or a stink horn, for instance. The spores fall to the ground or are carried off on air currents. If a spore lands on a suitable surface, it germinates and produces thread-like hyphae which begin to spread and find food.

Never eat or taste a mushroom or any other fungus unless an expert has told you that it is safe to do so.

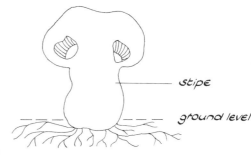

When the young mushroom first emerges, the cap is joined to the stipe (stalk) by a membrane or veil which protects the gills.

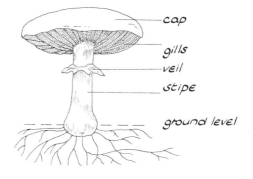

The cap extends fully & the veil ruptures to expose the gills.

CONIFEROUS WOODLAND

Coniferous woodlands are largely composed of trees belonging to the group of plants called Gymnosperms. This group includes pine, larch, spruce, cedar, yew and juniper.

Gymnosperm means naked seed; if you prise the scales of a mature cone apart, you will find that each one has one or two seeds developing on the upper surface of the scale. In contrast, the seeds of flowering plants (a large group called Angiosperms) are enclosed in pods, capsules, soft flesh or thick tissue.

Most conifers are cone bearing, but not all. Yew and juniper, for example, have berry-like fruits which are attractive to birds, who eat the flesh then void the seed away from the parent plant.

Not all conifers are evergreen. Larch is the most common deciduous conifer. In spring, when the delicate

Conifer seeds often have papery wings.

needles are opening, look for 'larch roses', the pink female flower-like cone structures of the larch.

Conifer trees grow quickly with straight trunks, making them a profitable crop. They are also able to grow on poor soils, so there are now so many conifer plantations in upland areas that they are replacing open moorland. The ability to grow successfully in soil which is poor in nutrients is partly due to the close relationship the roots have with a fungus, as described above. Conifer plantations are often fenced to keep sheep out; this gives grass, heather and bilberry a chance to grow among the young trees. Here heathland birds such as skylarks and meadow pipits nest, while short-eared owls hunt the field voles who live in the grass cover.

As the trees in the plantation grow, their branches begin to meet above the field layer. This shades out the ground cover plants, and the animals who have used them for food and shelter have to move away. At this 'thicket' stage of their growth, the conifers provide a home for birds who like to nest in these conditions. At an early thicket stage, birds such as yellowhammer, whitethroat and willow warbler will take advantage of the shelter offered. At a later stage, when the trees are taller, the nests of tits, goldcrests, chaffinches and song thrushes may be found.

When the conifers become tall trees, their side branches are cleared in order to promote knot-free timber. The cut branches are left on the ground to discourage any plants of the field layer from growing. Wrens may nest in the tangles of cut branches, while in the tree tops there may be the nests of crows, wood pigeons and long-eared owls.

Crossbills nest in conifers of various heights. These acrobatic birds have bills able to prise open the scales of cones to extract the seeds. They begin nesting in February to coincide with the ripening of conifer seeds.

Red deer, roe deer, red squirrel, pine marten, stoat, weasel, wild cat, fox and rabbit are among the mammals who live in the remains of pine forests.

The Scots pine is grown as a timber-producing conifer. It is an easy tree to identify. The blue-green needles are about 4 cm (1½ in) long, and are set in pairs into a little sheath at each base. As the parts of the upper trunk and branches reach about ten years of age, the grey outer bark falls off, to reveal a pinky-orange coloration.

Male and female reproductive structures are set on the same tree; they are like soft cones. There are many male cones (microsporophylls) set some way back from the shoot tips; each male cone is an upright spike with spirally arranged scales. Underneath each scale there are

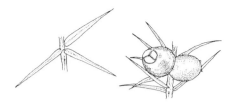

Juniper has purple berries. The sharp-pointed blue-green needles are in groups of three, set all around the stem.

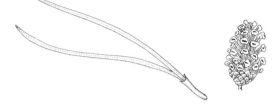

Pine needles are in pairs, threes or fives, held by a sheath at the base. Scots pine needles are in twos.

Female yew trees carry fleshy scarlet cups, or arils; each contains one black seed.

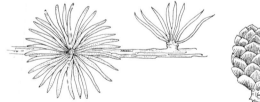

Larch, LARIX DECIDUA, is a deciduous conifer. The needles are in clusters of 20 to 30, springing from a woody knob.

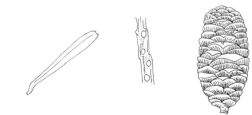

Fir needles have a flat, round base & leave a flat, round scar on the stem.

two pollen sacs which split to release spherical pollen grains, with two air sacs to increase their buoyancy and help in their dispersal by the wind.

There are fewer female cones (macrosporophylls); these appear at the tips of shoots, at the same time as the males develop further back. The female structure also has an upright spike with spirally arranged scales; some of these scales are small leaf-like bracts, which protect the egg-bearing (ovuliferous) scales during their development. At the base of each ovuliferous scale there are two egg cells (ovules).

In late spring or early summer, the ripe pollen is released. The female cones open their soft, pink scales to catch the wind-borne pollen. Each ovule releases a drop of fluid to hold any pollen that may enter between the scales. This 'pollination droplet' gradually dries, and as it does so the captured pollen grain is carried towards the egg cell; meanwhile the scales of the female cone close on the pollen grains.

Each pollen grain begins to grow a little tube; but it doesn't grow far at this stage, because during the autumn and winter it becomes dormant. Growth is resumed the following spring when the pollen tube penetrates the tissue surrounding the egg cell; now the male generative cell, carried by the tube, is able to fuse with the egg. Fertilization has taken place, about eleven months after pollination.

As the seeds develop, the surrounding scales become brown and woody. When the seeds are ready to be shed, the cone responds to atmospheric humidity: when the air is dry the scales move apart; when it is damp they close. The winged seeds are released on a dry day, when there is a good chance of their being carried away on a breeze.

Cone identification

a) Picea abies, *Norway spruce, Christmas tree*

b) Cupressus macrocarpa *Monterey cypress*

c) Thuja plicata, *western red cedar*

d) Tsuga canadensis, *eastern hemlock*

e) Pseudotsuga menziesii, *Douglas fir*

f) Larix decidua, *European larch*

Life-cycle of a Pine

a) *male cone*
b) *one of the scales*
c) *magnified pollen grain – note the air sacs*

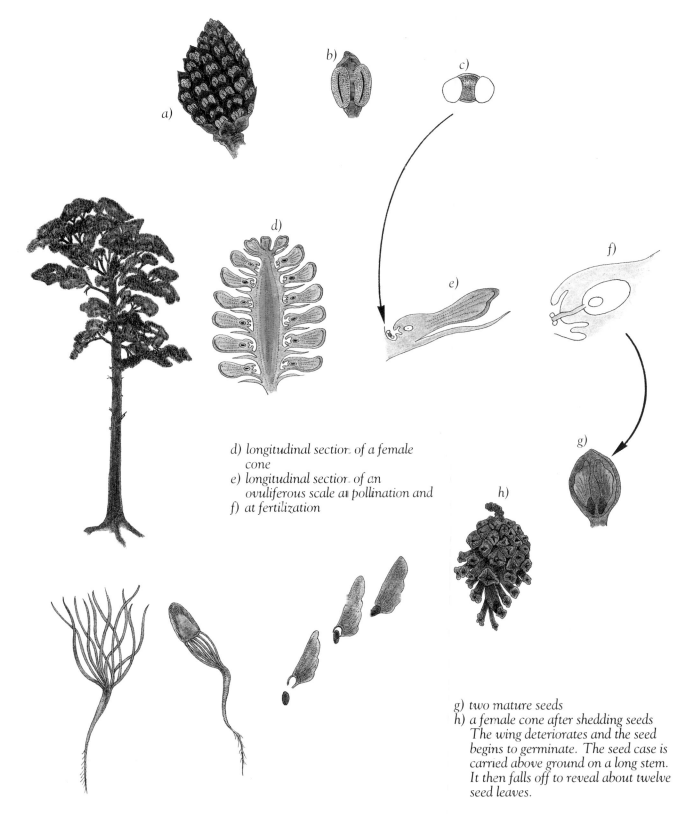

d) *longitudinal section of a female cone*
e) *longitudinal section of an ovuliferous scale at pollination and*
f) *at fertilization*

g) *two mature seeds*
h) *a female cone after shedding seeds The wing deteriorates and the seed begins to germinate. The seed case is carried above ground on a long stem. It then falls off to reveal about twelve seed leaves.*

Winter Survival

Holly berries

Although autumn brings shorter days and heralds the season of long nights, I still enjoy it. I love swishing through multi-coloured fallen leaves, and inevitably finding those perfect ones that are so beautiful they have to be taken home and pressed; to be found weeks later, falling out of a book, bringing with them the memory of the smell of leaf mould and bonfires.

Autumn is also the time for fruits: shiny apples, luscious blackberries, bright rosehips and necklaces of black bryony, cascading through the hedgerow in a glow of gold, orange and scarlet. Acorns roll free from their cups, beech nuts spill from their velvety nests and polished mahogany conkers hide under leaves or stay hidden inside their hedgehog-like cases, waiting for that moment of discovery when their beauty is first revealed. Then there are the cobwebs, those ethereal, dew-spangled works of art, spread sparkling in the crisp morning air.

Strange and colourful fungi appear overnight in woodlands and on grassland: the red-brown glow of brittle caps, the golden-yellow of orange pholiota and the deep-purple russula with its subtle apple scent. The meadow wax-cap spreads its tawny canopy in old meadows, and the scarlet hoods of *Hygrocybe coccinea* rise like jewels from spangled grass.

Many birds leave their summer haunts and fly southwards. Their going may pass unnoticed, until one day we realize that swallows, martins or swifts no longer swoop overhead. While some birds leave, others return; many to estuarine habitats which attract migrant birds from their northern summer breeding grounds. The sight of flocks of dunlin, knot, curlew, sandpiper and the little stint, is unforgettable.

One of the most exciting sounds of autumn must be the honking of wild geese or swans migrating. Their contact calls keep the families within the flocks together as they wing their way to their traditional wintering grounds.

Autumn is a time of preparation, a time for plants and animals to get ready for the winter season ahead, when temperatures may be very low and food hard to come by.

Fruits of the alder

PREPARING FOR WINTER

In autumn we can see how some plants prepare for winter. Many trees drop their leaves, while herbaceous plants cut off food supplies to all parts that show above the ground, then survive the winter months by using the food stored in their roots. Potatoes, carrots, parsnips and beetroots are all root storage organs.

Some plants produce seeds which will not germinate unless they have spent a period of time in the cold. Look at the instructions on seed packets: some seeds have to be put into the fridge for a while before they are sown. Other plants produce seeds that germinate better if they have passed through an animal undigested; the stomach enzymes soften the hard seed coat (testa), enabling the root and shoot to break through.

The droppings of animals show the importance of fruit in their diet; voles, mice, hedgehogs, squirrels, foxes, badgers and many birds gather the harvest of fruits. Some birds and mammals look for harder fruits such as acorns and beech mast. Nuts have the advantage of being durable, so they can be stored for the whole winter.

Jays and rooks collect acorns and carry them away from the parent tree before disgorging them one by one from their crop and burying them. Nuthatches embed their nut stores in the crevices of trees. Thrushes and blackbirds usually build their nests up to a metre (3 ft) from the ground, so that the old nests become perfect store cupboards for mice and voles who climb up with their fruits. Grey and red squirrels keep caches of nuts in many places. Some of the stored nuts are hidden away so well that they are not found; then they begin to grow far away from the parent tree, often expanding the habitat.

If a plant or animal is going to survive and reproduce successfully, it has to fit in with its environment; if it does not, it will cease to exist. This fitting in is known as adaptation. The study of any animal or plant will show adaptations to the environment, but no matter how well an organism is adapted it may still have to make adjustments to its internal state to counteract any changes in its environment. The more obvious environmental changes are those of increasing or decreasing temperature, and the shortening or lengthening of daylight hours.

Only birds and mammals are able to maintain a temperature constantly higher than their surroundings. Invertebrates, fish, amphibians and reptiles are 'cold blooded': their body temperature fluctuates with that of their surroundings.

A squirrel begins at the base of a cone & strips off the scales to get at the seeds. A squirrel often has a favourite feeding place, where there are many stripped cones.

A vole has short legs & so holds a nut with the base close to its back feet. After gnawing a hole in the shell, it puts its nose & mouth inside the nut to eat, leaving no teeth marks.

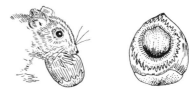

A woodmouse has longer legs & holds the nut at an angle. Only the bottom teeth gnaw the nut, while the top teeth hold & turn - leaving teeth marks on the shell.

In an uncongenial environment, animals have four options: to emigrate, to migrate, to adapt or to die.

Many animals emigrated southwards from northern Europe when the ice sheets covered the land; and some have not returned.

Migration is a long-distance mass movement – usually from a breeding ground to a feeding ground, the return journey being made as the breeding season approaches. The annual pattern of many birds is to fly southwards in autumn and northwards in spring. Cuckoos, warblers, swallows and white storks are among the birds who undertake the long, arduous journey from Europe to central or southern Africa. Brent, white-fronted and barnacle geese from Greenland overwinter in Ireland and south west Scotland, while those from Russia choose to fly to north western Europe. France, Britain and Ireland play host to fieldfares, redwings, song thrushes, blackbirds, starlings and bramblings who fly west or west-south-west to comparatively warmer climes. Duck fly to the Danish islands or to the west of Britain in their thousands; water fowl and wading birds of all sorts look for ice-free water and mud-flats, where they are able to feed in winter.

Animals which do not migrate adapt to the changes in their environment. Here are a number of ways used by animals to help them through the winter.

Diapause is a state of delayed development, or suspended animation, during the life of some invertebrates. It takes place at a particular stage of development which varies with the species. The vapourer moth overwinters as an egg, the yellow underwing as a caterpillar and the dagger moth in pupation. The state of diapause can become fixed in a life-cycle where it occurs every generation; however, where there are two generations a year, as for instance in the case of the holly blue butterfly, diapause only takes place during the winter months.

Many cold blooded animals adopt a form of seasonal acclimatization called torpor. This state involves the supercooling of body fluids, made possible by the release of chemicals into the fluids to stop them freezing, in the way that anti-freeze works in a car radiator. Many caterpillars overwinter in this way; so do queen wasps and bumble bees, butterflies, slugs and snails. Look under logs and slabs for overwintering snails; you will see that they have made a hard shutter across the entrance to their shell to keep the cold out.

Hibernation is the word most often used to describe the winter dormancy of mammals. Dormice are the only true hibernating mammals in Britain, where they sleep

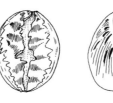

Young squirrels leave many teeth marks on nut shells. Older squirrels have more experience & so leave only a few short teeth marks on top of the nut shell.

Leaf miners are the larvae of tiny moths. The serpentine mines are very narrow at first, but broaden out as the larva grows fatter on the nutritious leaf tissue.

from the end of September through to spring. Hedgehogs and bats sleep very deeply, but they are easily roused by noise, warmth or extreme cold. Each time they wake from their deep sleep they use up a great deal of energy, so a long, cold winter is better for these animals than a winter with warm spells. Squirrels and badgers sleep through periods of bad weather to save energy.

Mammals begin to grow thicker coats as the days grow shorter in autumn; the extra fur helps to combat the cold. You will have noticed this happening to domestic pets – or maybe you notice them losing their extra fur in the lengthening days of spring! Birds fluff out their feathers on cold days, making themselves look like pompoms with legs.

LEAF COLOUR IN AUTUMN

Plants must overcome the harsh weather conditions too. The green colour in plants is caused by the presence of two closely related pigments, chlorophyll 'a' and chlorophyll 'b'. These pigments only form in the leaf in the presence of light; plants kept in total darkness lose their green colour and do not renew the pigments as long as they are in the dark. You can prove this point by putting a houseplant away in a cupboard, but be warned – it may never be the same again!

Plants not only need light to form chlorophyll, the temperature must be favourable too: chlorophyll does not form at temperatures lower than 2° C (36° F) or higher than 40° C (104° F). They also need an adequate supply of water, minerals and carbohydrates. Water and minerals are taken from the soil through the roots, and carbohydrates are manufactured in the plant's leaves.

Chlorophyll pigments are necessary to the plant for photosynthesis to take place; this is the method by which organic foods are manufactured from simple inorganic compounds, using light energy. The four factors necessary for photosynthesis are sunlight, chlorophyll in living cells, carbon dioxide and water. The end products of this manufacturing process are oxygen, carbohydrates and water vapour – essential components for life.

The green leaves of many trees and shrubs begin to take on their autumn coloration with the lengthening hours of darkness and the coming of colder temperatures, marking the end of the growing season. An abscission layer is formed at the base of the leaf in autumn; the cells behind this layer become corky and impervious to water. The transport of materials in and out of the leaf becomes

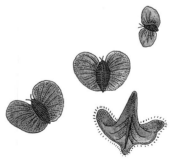

Silver birch fruits

133

impeded, and this interferes with the formation of chlorophyll. Chlorophyll is continually destroyed by sunlight, and when the supplies required for its renewal run out the leaves quickly lose their green colour.

When the green colour disappears, any other colouring matter which may be present can be seen.

Yellow flavenoids and orange and orange-red carotenoids are colours associated with autumn leaves. The yellow colours are always found in association with chlorophyll in leaves, protecting the chlorophyll from too much sunlight; so when the green can no longer be produced the yellow becomes visible. These colours are more stable in sunlight than chlorophyll and so they persist in the leaves. Trees such as ash, horse chestnut, poplar, birch and sycamore have predominantly yellow leaves in autumn.

The chlorophyll which makes fruits green when unripe is eliminated in the same way as it is in the leaves. Pears, lemons, grapefruits, carrots, apricots, oranges, rosehips and some peppers are yellow, orange and orange-red when they are ready to eat.

Chlorophyll does not boil out of leaves, but it may be extracted by putting a lightly boiled leaf into alcohol. Isopropyl alcohol can be bought in chemists.

It is a solvent, so guard it well.

Poplar (above) *and sycamore* (left) *have predominantly yellow leaves in autumn, while some oaks turn bright red.*

The red colours which appear in autumn vegetation are caused by pigments which are often not previously present in the leaf, but are formed when it begins to decline. The red pigments are anthocyanins – chemical compounds which give plants the colours red, blue and violet-purple. Very often the leaves which develop the greatest intensity of red are rich in carbohydrates in the form of monosaccharides – sugars. Coloration is usually richest in seasons when there is an abrupt change from high summer temperatures to low autumn ones, so that the movement of sugars out of the leaf is suddenly retarded. Maples, sumac, some oak trees and Virginia creeper have red autumn leaves.

Blackberries, bilberries, blackcurrants and beetroots are red-purple when they are ripe; and the colour stains your fingers when you split the skins and allow the juice out. Anthocyanins are water soluble, so can be extracted by boiling or by using alcohol. Boil leaves that are usually red-purple to reveal the chlorophyll, which may then be extracted by using alcohol.

LEAF FALL

Autumn leaf fall is a characteristic of deciduous trees and shrubs. Evergreens such as holly, laurel and pine keep their leaves for an indefinite period; but some of the older leaves of evergreens are shed at some time during the year.

All land plants give out water vapour by a process called transpiration. You can observe this by putting a pot plant into a plastic bag and tying the opening of the bag firmly around the plant stem above soil level. In about half an hour, moisture from the leaves will have formed droplets inside the bag.

Transpiration can take place from any exposed part of the plant, but the greatest water loss is through the stomata – the pores – in the leaves. The transpiration rate is not constant; it varies with conditions in the atmosphere as well as with conditions inside the plant. The rate increases in windy or warm weather, but decreases in high humidity. The plant loses less water at night because the stomata close in darkness.

Unfortunately the plant has no control over its stomata; they are governed by chemical and physical conditions within the plant. At times the loss of water can be very harmful and the plant is unable to help itself. So plants have had to make adaptations to help them survive adverse conditions, such as winter.

The leaves of evergreen trees have fewer stomata than the leaves of deciduous trees, and the covering of the leaf is much thicker and quite waxy. You can feel this difference if you take a holly leaf in one hand and an oak leaf in the other. The holly leaf is tough and shiny and the oak leaf is thin and matt.

On frosty days in winter, the water in the soil is often frozen, so plants cannot take it up; yet the sun may be shining and the temperature quite warm, so the

Below is a diagrammatic representation of the junction of a leaf stalk and a twig. (Continued overleaf.)

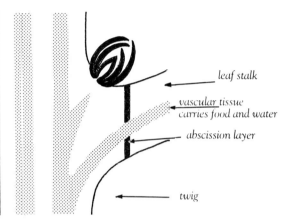

leaf stalk

vascular tissue carries food and water

abscission layer

twig

c) *Towards the end of the growing season, the cells at the base of the leaf stalk divide and form layers of cells across the region where the leaf stalk joins the twig. The layers of cells nearest to the twig are corky; the layers nearest to the leaf stalk are thin-walled and loosely packed. This is the abscission layer.*

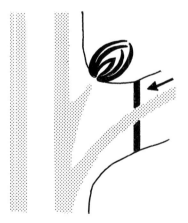

b) *Valuable substances made by the leaf are broken down into soluble form and are passed into the plant to be stored.*

135

transpiration rate is high. Under these conditions, the leaves of deciduous trees would soon wilt and the plant would die from lack of water. The process of leaf fall prevents this from happening.

Towards the end of the growing season, the cells at the base of the leaf stalk divide and form layers across the area where the leaf stalk joins the twig. The layers of cells nearest to the twig are corky, the layers nearest to the leaf stalk are thin-walled and loosely packed. This is the abscission layer.

The valuable carbohydrates made by the leaf are in soluble form and are passed into the plant to be stored. Waste substances are passed from the plant to the leaf for excretion. The cork cells now block the vascular tissue; water and minerals are no longer able to enter the leaf from the plant.

The cells in the leaf and the leaf stalk now degenerate. The vascular strands, which once carried the plant's water and food supplies to and from the leaf, finally break and the leaf falls. The abscission layer protects the plant from water loss and prevents the entry of disease-producing organisms.

The shape of the scar left by the leaf is specific for a given species of plant. Look at a twig of horse chestnut: the leaf scars are horseshoe shaped, the vein scars are like the nails in a shoe.

What happens to the leaves that fall in autumn? In a woodland or under a hedgerow, most of the plant material found on the ground will be broken down by decomposers. Most land plants contain a supporting material, to stiffen their parts and hold them up; this is usually cellulose or lignin. These substances have to be broken down by specialist feeders with special digestive enzymes – stomach juices – which break down tough material. Bacteria and fungi do this job by pouring enzymes on to their food and absorbing the digested matter directly into their bodies. This process takes place very quickly in moist conditions, and raw materials are released into the soil.

This is the action that takes place in a compost heap; the white threads you find there are the fungal threads, or hyphae. The bacteria are too small for you to see, but you can feel the warmth of their activity.

Some soil animals, such as earthworms, insects, insect larvae and many other invertebrates, feed directly on fallen leaves, seeds and the general plant debris found in the leaf litter layer. Leaves may be pulled down into the soil by earthworms who enjoy eating the tender tips. If you look around your lawn or grassy places, you may see the ends of leaves sticking out of the ground; this means

c) *Waste substances are passed from the plant into the leaf for excretion. Cork cells now block the vascular tissue; water and minerals no longer enter the leaf from the plant.*

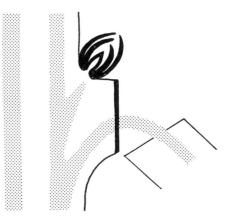

d) *The cells in the leaf and leaf stalk degenerate. The vascular strands finally sever and the leaf falls. The abscission layer protects the plant from water loss and from the entry of disease-producing organisms.*

that the other bits are being feasted upon below ground.

So, follow the fate of a fallen leaf. It has holes nibbled in it by tiny animals such as springtails, fly larvae, bristletails and bark lice; then bacteria and fungi begin their work. Pauropods, proturans, tiny larvae and other members of the soil and leaf litter community chew the weakened tissue; then slugs, snails, woodlice and millipedes join in and skeletonize the leaf. At this stage, when the surface area has increased, the maximum bacterial action takes place and the leaf decomposes into the soil, where earthworms continue the attack.

Earthworms excrete the wastes from the leaf remains and these become mixed in with the soil, increasing the mineral content; the soil is then loosened and mixed by the activities of burrowing animals, the earthworms playing a major role in these activities.

Under natural conditions, the wastes from one decomposer are used up as food by other decomposers. Waste not, want not!

Overleaf is an identification chart of autumn leaves.

The story of a fallen leaf

An autumn leaf falls

Holes are eaten into it by springtails & bark lice, then fungi & bacteria begin work.

Bristletails, fly larvae & other soil animals eat the leaf.

Millipedes, woodlice, snails & earwigs skeletonize the leaf.

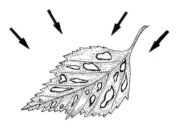

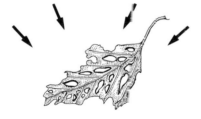

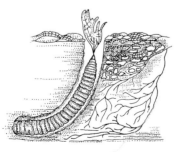

When the surface area has increased, maximum bacterial action takes place. Earthworms eat the fragments.

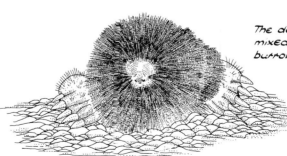

The decomposing material is mixed into the soil by burrowing & digging animals.

Scots pine needles grow in pairs. This tree is a conifer.

Lime, or linden, trees have heart-shaped leaves.

Look for nail galls on the leaves of the field maple.

Rowan, or mountain ash, shows yellow, orange or scarlet autumn colour.

Whitebeam leaves are silvery grey underneath.

The leaves of common hawthorn and of Midland hawthorn

Hornbeam leaves cling to the twigs for much of the winter.

Hazel trees carry brown, closed up catkins through the winter.

Beech leaves cling to the twigs through the winter months.

Look for the purse galls and spiral galls on the stems of fallen poplar leaves.

There may be bean galls on crack willow leaves.

Watch out for the fat buds of 'pussy' willow bursting in early spring.

Sycamore leaves may be marked by 'tar-blotch' fungus.

Horse chestnut twigs have fat, sticky buds in the spring.

Look for blotch mines on the evergreen leaves of holly.

Wych elm trees show a resistance to Dutch elm disease.

Silver birch trees have silver-grey and black trunks.

Alder trees have purple-brown club-shaped buds in winter.

Sweet chestnut leaves are red-gold in autumn.

Many brown sessile oak leaves cling to the twigs in winter.

The holm oak is evergreen.

The leaves of the London plane are similar to those of the sycamore.

Ash trees have black leaf buds.

Look for the light, white pith that forms in elder twigs.

Beachcombing

A seashore must be one of the most complex of environments, where twice daily changes overcome the shore life in the way that seasonal changes slowly overtake the plants and animals who live inland.

A seascape can change so quickly that the horizon may be clear and sharp one minute and blurred by a squall the next. A sea that is blue and gentle, with glistening ripples, can change in next to no time to a leaden grey with white horses galloping over steep waves.

Is it this unpredictability that draws us to the sea? Or is it the sight of the endless moving water, whose far, invisible edge is lapping on some distant shore, stirring our imagination? Maybe we hope to catch sight of one of the strange creatures of the deep, who live in a world so different from our own.

On the shore we can see a host of sea birds who dig for food in the wet sand left by the ebbing tide. Shrimps, starfish and small scuttling crabs enjoy the warmth and stillness of a rock pool, while beautiful, shining shells roll in and out of the sea edge before being left stranded.

For me the most exciting life to be found on the sea shore is in the inter-tidal zones, where slippery seaweeds glisten in the sun and barnacles encrust the edges of shining rock pools. It is fun to explore this area as the tide retreats, for who knows what strange treasures the sea will leave behind.

The diagram below shows how the 28-day rhythm of spring and neap tides is influenced by the sun and moon.

a) When the sun and the moon are pulling at an angle to each other, a smaller tide occurs. This is called a neap tide.

b) When the sun and moon pull together, they cause a high tide. This is called a spring tide and occurs about every two weeks.

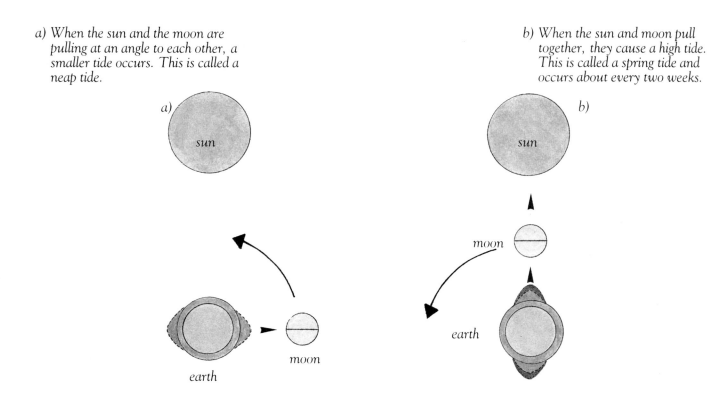

140

TIME AND TIDE WAIT FOR NO MAN

There are two tides a day; that is, two high tides and two low tides. The flood tide creeps slowly up the shore, and the ebb tide slowly recedes again. The highest point the sea reaches on the shore is called high water, and the lowest point low water; when the sea reaches low water and turns from ebb tide to flood tide, it takes about six hours and twelve and a half minutes to reach high water. The same happens at ebb tide, so each full tide takes twelve hours and 25 minutes. This means that the times of high and low tide change a little each day. Mediterranean tides and the tides of the Baltic Sea are hardly noticed, but those of other seas can't be missed.

Tides are caused by the gravitational pull of the sun and the moon upon the oceans. The moon slowly rotates in an elliptical orbit around the earth and, when the sun and the moon are in line and pulling together, the force is so strong that the tides are very high and are called spring tides. This name has nothing to do with the season; it comes from the Old English 'springen', to rise. There is, however, a seasonal effect as well; the highest spring tides occur when the moon is closest to the earth, at the March and September equinoxes. Spring tides do not only rise further up the shore than other tides, they also drop lower down, exposing more shore than usual. When the sun and the moon are at different angles, the gravitational pull is not so great and the tides are less extreme – these are neap tides. Spring tides occur every two weeks or so, near the times of the new and the full moon, while neap tides happen between the spring tides, after the first and third quarters of the moon.

The constantly changing sea level and water cover affect the plants and animals. Some are able to endure some time out of the water, but others are very sensitive to any exposure to high temperatures in summer, low temperatures in winter and the high radiation of sunlight at any time of the year.

At sea, plants and animals rise to just below the water surface to enjoy sunlight; on shore, sunlight is with them to some degree each day; but the food-bearing sea is only available from tide to tide. The area between low water and high water supports a well defined pattern of plants and animals, from those which only meet the sea when a spring tide brings high water, to those which are only exposed to view at the low water of a spring tide.

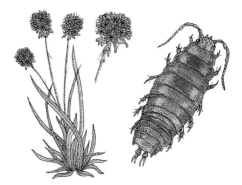

Thrift is a plant found tucked into rock crevices. The sea slater hides under stones or in crevices by day and emerges at night.

The horned poppy, below, grows on shingle beds. Bristletails are found in cracks and crevices high on the shore in the splash zone.

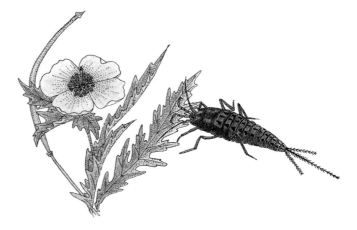

Top shells are common on rocky shores; mother of pearl shines through where the shell has worn thin. a) grey top shell from below; b) painted top shell; c) purple top shell; d) thick top shell.

a)

b)

c)

d)

THE ZONES OF A ROCKY SHORE

The splash zone is the strip at the top of the shore that is only splashed by the waves when a spring tide reaches its peak. Orange and grey land lichens and black sea lichens grow on the rocks in this area, forming finely cracked crusts over the rocks.

The high water spring tide zone leaves a line of driftwood and seaweed, and there are many interesting things to find. I enjoy looking for cuttlefish bone, 'mermaids' purses' and clusters of common whelk egg shells in this zone. A variety of creatures such as beetles, flesh flies, and small worms feed on the jetsam, alongside the host of sand hoppers who leap and bound over the decaying debris in the evenings, seeming to show an uncontained joy of life.

The high water neap tide line marks the lower edge of the upper zone of the shore; look for seaweeds such as the olive-green channel wrack, which becomes black and brittle when it is dry. Rough winkles (periwinkles), with their rough sculptured shells, are found on this part of the shore. Here they give birth to fully developed young, tiny replicas of their parents. The adults have gills which absorb oxygen from damp air, so they are able to colonize this zone happily. Small winkles, the smallest of the periwinkles, live in this zone too, roosting in rows in slits

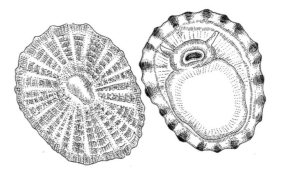

Limpets have a strong foot which acts as a suction pad, holding the animal firmly to rocks & protecting it from predators & rough seas. Underneath you can see the animal's head, mouth & tentacles.

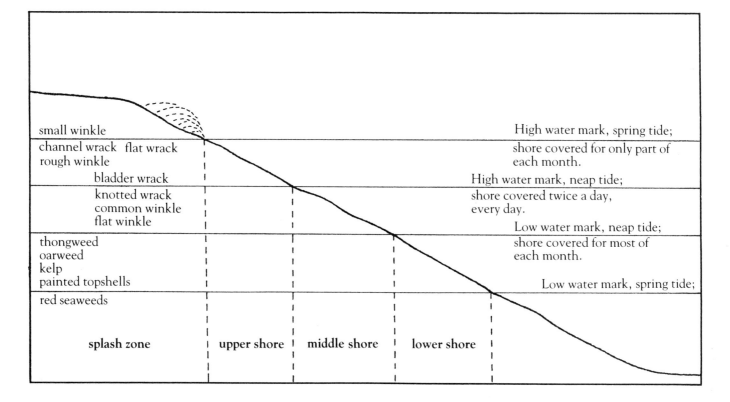

In this sea shore picture we look over
the plants of shingle and dune to see a
few of the birds often seen by the sea.

From left to right the plants are: long-horned popy, sea
spurrey, sea holly, sea campion, rock samphire, common
scurvygrass, thrift, sea aster, sea bindweed and burnet
rose. Red admiral butterflies are often seen in coastal areas
as these strong flying insects migrate northwards from the
Mediterranean, spreading throughout Europe and reaching
Britain and Ireland.

The shells washed up on the beach include top shells,
trough shells, tellins and periwinkles.

The birds are: puffins with their brightly coloured bills; a
common tern, with a black cap and long tail streamers; a
common gull flies in the centre with a little gull soaring
above and a kittiwake gliding in from the right. In the
foreground a black and white oyster-catcher stands on one
leg being watched by two knots in their summer plumage;
while on the right a ringed plover patters its feet on the
ground to encourage food to reveal itself.

143

and crevices in the rocks. Small winkles release their eggs into the sea, where the larvae become members of the plankton for a while.

The middle zone has the brown seaweeds, bladder and knotted wrack. These are the seaweeds with poppable, gas-filled bladders; the bladders keep the plants buoyant in the sea, exposing them to plenty of light. Common and flat winkles, mussels, barnacles and thick top shells live on the rocks of the middle shore zone, where twice a day the sea brings them food. The dog whelk, a carnivorous snail, prowls among the barnacles. Having selected dinner, the whelk proceeds to soften the shell of the unfortunate mollusc with acid and bores into the shell with its toothed radula; the soft flesh is then carried back along the conveyor-belt of teeth into the throat of the whelk. Dog whelks also eat mussels if they are plentiful. It is possible to tell which of these foods a whelk has been eating by the colour of its shell; a pale shelled whelk has been eating barnacles, while a dark brown or mauve-pink shell indicates a diet of mussels.

The low water zone has the low neap tide line as its top boundary, and the low spring tide line as its bottom boundary. Look for the strands of brown serrated wrack which often carry the coiled grey-white tubes of bristle worms; here, too, you will probably find oar weed and thong weed, which are thick-stemmed brown seaweeds; there may also be some red seaweeds in this zone. Painted top shells, mussels, velvet shells, limpets and dog whelks cling to the rocks of the lower shore; these animals either grip very firmly, or are able to roll about in the waves without being damaged.

A side view of a Norway lobster. Its underside is shown below.

Lug worms leave casts on sandy beaches. Shallow depressions mark the top of the lug worm's burrow.

144

THE ZONES OF A SANDY SHORE

Life upon and within a sandy shore presents a contrast to the rich variety of life on a rocky shore. A sandy shore does not provide a surface for attachment, so seaweeds are absent, as are all the small animals who shelter in and fasten themselves on to the fronds. Gone too are the squirts, sponges and sea anemones who need an anchorage, and the snails who creep on hard surfaces. Rocks provide shelter for crabs and various worms when the sea is beating against the shore, or if they are left behind by the ebbing tide; but there is no such shelter on a sandy shore. The animals who live in this situation are beneath the sand; they are burrowers.

Some, for example the lug worms, swallow large amounts of sand, digesting the organic contents and passing the sand back through the gut. You may have seen the coiled casts they leave behind on wet sand, or the depressions in the sand or mud where they have burrowed down. There are sand-dwellers such as cockles who, when the tide is in, draw water into their siphons and strain out the nutritious plankton through the fine network of gills. Others, such as the sand masons (tube worms) and tellins (bivalves) are deposit feeders who live on the detritus of plant and animal origin, which collects on the surface of the sand. The most active of the sand-dwellers are the predators who hunt down the other sand animals. One of these is the cat-worm, a silvery white predator; another is a glycerid worm which coils round and round if disturbed.

On the tide line where loose seaweed is rolled up by the tide, the sandhoppers feed by night. They burrow into the dry sand each morning to hide away from the light; mother sandhoppers, carrying eggs or with young in their brood pouch, do not emerge from their burrows to join the excited nightly gambols of the others. Common shrimps also burrow in the sand to hide by day, while by night they walk sedately over the sand searching for food. You have probably seen shrimps for sale, with their transparent stomachs packed with bits of green plants. Others have yellowy-coloured stomach contents; these are probably ingested eggs, young stages of fish or smaller crustaceans.

Sea kale is a large cabbage-like plant found on shingly beaches. Sand hoppers are found amongst the seaweed on the strand line.

The common whelk has a sensitive siphon with which it detects its food.
Fully developed young emerge from the sponge-like masses of egg capsules.

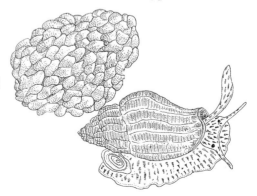

Burrowing animals

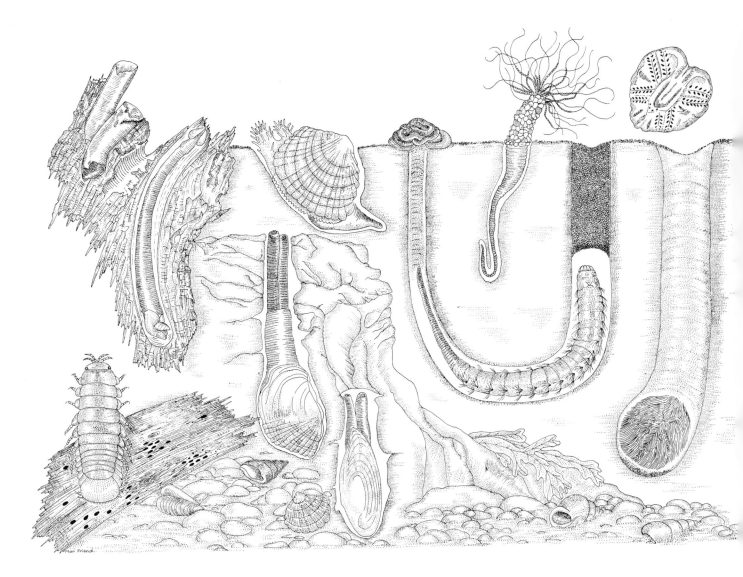

Look from left to right in this picture & find the following: a gribble & a shipworm in wood; an oval piddock & a flask shell in rock; an edible cockle; a lugworm in its burrow with a sand mason above; a sea potato in the sand with a test, or skeleton, above; a common tellin filtering food from the sand, with a Baltic tellin & a small cockle 'asleep' in the sand below. A razor shell burrowing down & a marine bristle worm - PECTINARIA - fishes for food in a cavity, safe in its tube of sand granules. The sand gaper is a soft-shelled clam which, once settled in sand or mud, spends a motionless life filtering suspended particles from the sea. This burrowing sea cucumber has minute, anchor-shaped spicules protruding through its soft skin, enabling it to move along & making it sticky to the touch. Under the sea cucumber is an acorn worm. These worms live in U-shaped burrows; they are filter feeders & extract food particles from the sea water. Under the acorn worm there is a ragworm; it has four eyes & strong jaws for feeding & burrowing. A tusk shell protrudes from the sand; this is a small sea mollusc who feeds in this 'upside down' position. Last of all is a banded wedge shell.

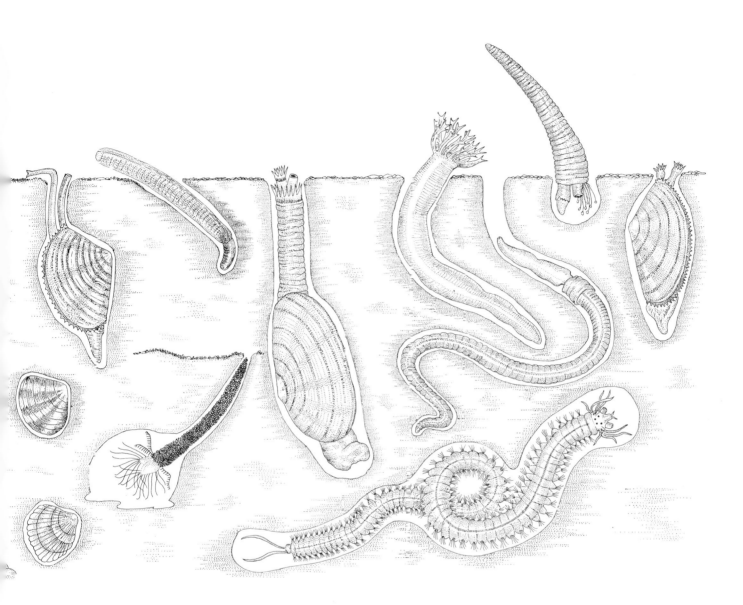

On an open sandy or muddy beach there are no rocks or seaweeds where animals can hide; the only safe place for them is in the sand itself. Sand-dwelling animals find their food in four different ways. Suspension feeders, including the common cockle, filter phytoplankton from the sea water; deposit feeders, such as the tellin, take food from the surface of the sand. These two feeding methods are possible when the tide is in. The third group, which includes the lugworm, eats the sand, digests the contained organic debris & evacuates the sand through the gut. The last group are the carnivores who prey on the other sand-dwellers; these include the white worm & the masked crab.

Shipworms have shells which have been reduced to highly specialized boring tools, attached to the end of a long worm-like body. They live & feed inside timber in sea water, while the woodlouse-like gribble burrows into timber that has been cast ashore. Piddocks & flask shells burrow into soft rock & firm clay; having found a comfortable place, they are content to stay there to feed & reproduce.

PLANKTON PASTURES

Vast numbers of tiny plants and animals float near the surface of fresh or salt waters, where they are able to take advantage of the sunlight. The plants in this water zone are called phytoplankton, and the animals are zooplankton, but they are usually grouped together simply as plankton.

Phytoplankton use the carbon dioxide produced by zooplankton, and take nutrients directly from the surrounding water, absorbing the phosphates and nitrates which surround them. Meanwhile zooplankton eat phytoplankton and use the oxygen they produce.

Both plant and animal plankton have some power of movement. Otherwise they would sink and die. Some have fats in their body tissues to buoy them up; some have spines or feather-like flagella to enable them to tread water; and some of the animals propel themselves by muscular force.

The pastures of plankton have seasons, the major influences being changes in day length and the surrounding temperature. In spring the plants multiply in the lengthening days and in summer, when the animals of the sea reproduce, many of their young join the plankton community as larvae. The larvae of worms, crustaceans, starfish, molluscs, fish and many others begin their lives drifting with the plankton, feeding on the plants or small animals surrounding them. Many of these larvae are themselves eaten, but the object is for the larvae to be dispersed before settling down to life in a small area or fastened to a rock, in adult form.

In autumn, when the gales bring nutrient-rich debris to the surface, the plants have a second flush. Winter is the testing time when only the fittest survive; the dead then drift down to the sea bed, where the detritus feeders eat them up.

If you take a trip in a fishing boat, trail a fine nylon net in the sea for a few minutes. The net will have some sludgy slime in it if nothing else! Put the net into a bowl of clean sea water so that the slime drifts free; then you should see it come to life with tiny animals jumping and darting in the water. It is even more wonderful if you are able to look at a drop through the microscope – then you will see the transparent, single-celled diatoms and dinoflagellates waving thread-like whiplash flagella in order to maintain depth.

These acorn barnacles are crustaceans – a group that includes crabs & prawns. When the tide is in, the animal extends feathery legs through the top of the shell, to catch food particles.

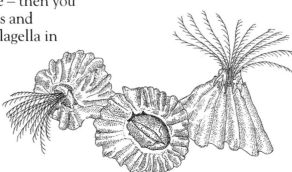

THE EDGE OF THE SEA

Many of us enjoy walking along the edge of the sea, cooling our feet on the wet sand and feeling the cold waves finish their energetic rolling with little ripples round our ankles.

Have you ever seen a swarm of sea gooseberries riding the ripples, and often being left stranded by the tide? Sea gooseberries sound delicious, but they are not edible; they are the most commonly seen of the comb jellies. They are globular, gelatinous, plum-shaped animals with two long tentacles, one on either side of the body. Sea gooseberries move forward, mouth foremost, by means of eight rows of cilia or 'combs', which are like fringes of threads, running from the apex to just short of the bottom of the animal; the threads all beat in rhythm. The hanging tentacles act like fishing rods and can be expanded to ten times the length of the sea gooseberry, or completely retracted into pouches.

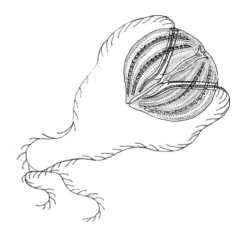

The sea gooseberry is a comb jelly with many small, beating, iridescent 'combs' running in rows down the body. The long tentacles trail in the sea like fishing lines.

The sea gooseberry is a voracious carnivore feeding on small crustaceans, small fish and larvae. The prey is caught on adhesive cells which line the tentacles; the victims are then wiped into the mouth. If you haven't seen a sea gooseberry before, it would be easy to think you had found some sort of light bulb, because the gastric canal system, seen through the transparent body, looks rather like the filaments of a bulb. Strangely enough a swarm of these animals, seen in the sea at night, lights up the area in an impressive display of luminescence.

Jellyfish are more sinister than comb jellies. They come upon you unobserved, and seem to follow your legs as you try to get out of their way. Although jellyfish can swim, they are at the mercy of the water currents; their main control is in their ability to maintain their orientation and to move up and down in the sea by pulsations of the bell, which expands and contracts rather like an umbrella being opened and closed.

A common jellyfish has an umbrella-like body called a bell. Fine stinging tentacles hang from the edge of the bell and frilly tentacles push stunned prey into the central mouth.

We mostly see the common jellyfish stranded on the sand, or in the sea close to the shore. It is 25 cm (10 in) or more in diameter with a transparent, blue-tinged, umbrella-shaped body. Around the edges of the umbrella shape, there is a fringe of short tentacles all equipped with stinging cells. Underneath the body there are four frilly arms which hang down around the mouth; this is the only way in and out of the body.

Jellyfish wait for prey to come within reach of their tentacles, which are armed with powerful stinging cells. The prey is stunned by the stings and is then passed to the oral arms, which in turn manoeuvre the comatose body into the mouth of the jellyfish. The stinging cells of

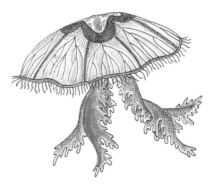

a jellyfish really hurt. I was once stung while swimming; it was like being stabbed with hot needles, and the pain went on and on. Even stranded jellyfish can inflict wounds, so, as with many things, it is better to look at them with your eyes and not with your hands.

Another sea animal with very powerful stings is the Portuguese man o' war, usually carried in the warm currents of the Gulf Stream. The Portuguese man o' war is really a colony of animals made up of four different types of individuals called polyps. The only part of the colony to be seen above water is the float, looking like an inflated plastic bag, pale pink or blue in colour and about 30 cm (12 in) long. Under the float hang feeding polyps, the polyps that fish for food, and others that defend and sting. As the Portuguese man o' war drifts along, its longest tentacles hang down 2.5 metres (8 ft) or so like a drift net to trap and sting prey before passing it to the mouths of the feeding polyps. In this strange co-operative animal, the fourth group of polyps is concerned with reproduction; eggs and sperm are released into the sea in a rather haphazard way that seems to work, and fertilized eggs produce larvae which eventually found further colonies.

Starfish can be found on the sea edge, in rock pools or stranded on the sand; the one usually found is the common starfish, *Asterias rubens*.

The body has a central disc, which carries the main organs and the five radial arms. Underneath the body, in the centre of the disc, is the mouth; and directly opposite, on the upper side of the body, is the anus. Underneath each arm, along a central avenue, there are two rows of hydraulic tube feet, with suctorial pads for gripping. These feet work in a unique way: they are driven by muscular power plus the fluid pressure of sea water inside the starfish. A sieve plate near the mouth admits the correct amount of sea water into the system; this flows along a channel to a canal that encircles the disc. From this ring canal, a radial canal radiates into each of the five arms; all the way along the canal there are little muscular sacs which connect with the hollow tube feet. To extend one of the tube feet, the sac is squeezed and water is forced into the tube foot, which extends it; when the suction pad at the end of the tube foot attaches itself to a surface, the foot contracts, forcing water back into the sac. All the little feet under the rays take tiny steps in the same direction, and the starfish is able to move several centimetres (an inch or more) a minute.

Starfish have a well developed sense of smell, by which they hunt their food of oysters, mussels and

The Portuguese man o' war, with its blue gas-filled bladder, floats along carried by the wind and tide. A sea gooseberry moves through the water by beating the combs which run in rows down the body. The compass jellyfish usually drifts with the currents, but is able to expand and contract the bell to propel itself along slowly. These animals all 'fish' for food as they travel along.

scallops. It is difficult to open one of these bivalve animals if it doesn't want to open, and it is hard to believe that a starfish can do with its tube feet that which we cannot do with our fingers. Bivalves can't move very much; and when the starfish chooses its prey it wraps itself round the victim, attaching some of the tiny tube feet to each valve. It then begins to exert a steady tension on the valves, and after some time the animal inside begins to tire and relaxes slightly. This allows the starfish to open the shells a very little, and that is all it needs. The starfish stomach is then extruded and inserted between the valves of its victim; when the stomach enzymes come into contact with the soft, live tissues of the prey, digestion begins.

Sea urchins belong to the same group of animals as starfish; in fact if you can visualize lifting each arm of a starfish to a point above its disc, and further imagine the arms connected, then you will see how a globular sea urchin is formed.

The shell, or test, of a sea urchin is about 10 cm (4 in) in diameter. It is covered with movable spines on ball and socket joints; these protect the sea urchin from predators and also help it to move around. The spines soon break off when the animal dies, leaving a pattern of little white knobs where they were attached. Among the spines are pincer-like blades on stalks; these keep the test free of detritus and small animals such as barnacle larvae, which would settle there given the chance. There are also tube feet interspersed among the spines. These work like those of a starfish; the pattern of the feet can be traced as holes on the empty test of the dead animal. The sea urchin's mouth and teeth are on the underside of its body; they are in the shape of a lantern, and the organ is called Aristotle's lantern. Sea urchins are vegetarians.

Have you ever seen the stalked barnacles which are often found attached to driftwood? These are goose barnacles, and they live in warm seas; they are so called because the stalk and shell are shaped like a goose's head and neck. When the goose barnacles are in the sea, their feather-like feeding filters wave around in the water, fishing. For hundreds of years it was thought that these barnacles were the young of the barnacle goose, as their goslings were never seen; it wasn't then known that their breeding grounds were north of the Arctic Circle. Put simply, the myth said, 'Barnacle geese develop from shell fish; the little geese cling to driftwood by their beaks as barnacles; and when large enough, they fly free as geese.' The clerics of the Middle Ages believed that if the barnacle goose began life in the sea it must be classified as a fish and could, therefore, be eaten on Fridays!

Necklace shells are rounded & shiny. The foot of the snail-like occupant is large & expands around the shell when the animal is on the move. Eggs are laid in spirally wound collars of jelly embedded with sand grains.

Starfish move slowly by means of rows of tube feet under each arm. They are very powerful and are able to open the shells of mussels and oysters, which they eat.

Sea urchins graze tiny animals from rocks and seaweeds. When the animal dies, the skeleton, or test, has white tubercles where the spines were attached and rows of holes where the tube feet protruded.

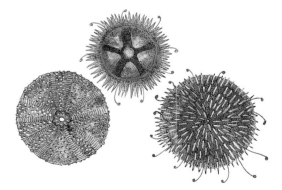

CAUGHT IN A ROCK POOL

When I go to a beach, I always look around for a rock pool. Kneeling down and gazing into the beautiful under-sea garden with its swimming, darting or creeping inhabitants is a wonderful treat.

Shrimps and prawns live on an assortment of food, from bits of seaweed and dead creatures to small live prey. Shrimps are mainly nocturnal, but prawns are usually to be seen swimming in a rock pool, beating the water with five pairs of swimming legs and streamlining their body by tucking up the ten walking legs and bending back the feelers. The prawn swims slowly along, scavenging for food, but you only have to draw your finger over the water surface to see it shoot backwards, paddling hard with its tail fan and darting away. I have been lucky enough to see a prawn moulting; they have to shed their exoskeleton every two weeks or so in the summer. The outgrown shell splits down the back, then the prawn humps its back and pushes outwards. It takes about two days for its new shell to harden, which is a long time to be vulnerable when predators lurk all around and could strike at any moment.

One way to tell a prawn from a shrimp is to look at its pincers. The common prawn has the largest pair of pincers on the second pair of walking legs, while the common shrimp has the largest pincers on the first pair of walking legs. Also, the common prawn has a beak, or rostrum, sticking forward out of the head between the eyes, but shrimps have only a small point or none at all.

During the summer, lobsters tend to move to shallower waters and they may occasionally be seen lurking in rock pools. It is more usual to see the tough, aggressive shore crab. This crab is resistant to exposure, and so can live not only in rock pools but also under stones and in cracks and crevices well up the shore. Adult shore crabs are dark green, but the young may be quite colourful: red, yellow and green with white patches, the colours varying from crab to crab.

The crabs I enjoy watching most are hermit crabs; they live in rocky places and shallow water. Like all crabs, the hermit crab has a tough exterior, but instead of a large carapace it has a soft and vulnerable abdomen, so it has to protect and conceal its delicate parts by adopting an empty shell. A winkle or whelk shell will do, but the crab explores the inside thoroughly before tucking its body carefully into the inner coils of the shell.

This idea works well until the crab grows too big for the shell. All animals with an external skeleton have a growth problem anyway, because when they shed their

Shore crabs hide beneath seaweed and stones. The female carries her orange-coloured eggs beneath a flap on her abdomen.

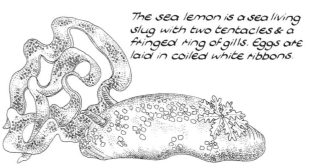

The sea lemon is a sea living slug with two tentacles & a fringed ring of gills. Eggs are laid in coiled white ribbons.

outer skin-like shell they are defenceless until the new one hardens; but the poor old hermit crab finds the process far more complicated. First he must squeeze himself out of his adopted shell, then moult, then return to his shell; but when he has moulted and expanded he often finds his shell is too small. If so, then he has to find an empty shell of just the right size.

We once kept some tropical land hermit crabs, and we always provided a supply of larger shells in their tank. It was fascinating watching the fresh pink abdomen of a newly moulted crab being poked into an empty shell, to see whether the fit was good. Then we had to remember which crab was wearing whose cast-off shell!

The abdomen of a hermit crab isn't straight; it is coiled so that it fits snugly into the coils of a shell. The crab's nippers are unequal in size, because the adopted shell is asymmetrical; the right hand nipper is larger and is used to close off the entrance to the shell when the crab takes refuge inside. The second and third pair of walking legs have to be very strong to carry both the crab and the shell; perhaps this is why the hermit crab walks so slowly, and why it is unable to swim.

Maybe it is all these problems that make hermit crabs so bad-tempered and pugnacious, for they often fight amongst themselves. They live by eating sick or injured animals, or by scraping organisms from the rocks; but they are messy feeders and spray a lot of food particles around while eating. This untidy habit stands them in good stead, because one of the solutions to the difficult life the hermit crab leads is to form an association with

When the hermit crab is out of its shell it is very vulnerable. When it takes possession of an empty whelk shell the pugnacious crab blends into the habitat where it scavenges any organic debris it finds.

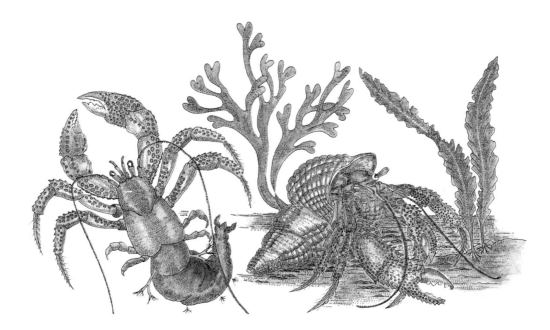

153

another organism that will help to protect it. There are several interesting domestic arrangements that can be made. Hermit crabs are often seen with one or more sea anemones living on their shell; the anemones eat the bits of food shed by the crab, and are then carried round to new feeding grounds, which is an advantage to a sedentary animal. In return, the anemones protect the crab from predators by using the stinging cells on their tentacles. When the hermit crab has to change shells, it stimulates the sea anemone in some way that persuades it to let go of the old shell and attach itself to the new. No one really knows how the crab induces the anemone to release its suction pad. It appears to stroke the anemone gently, but no amount of gentle stroking has ever moved a sea anemone for me – if anything, they cling tighter!

Sometimes a hermit crab will have a yellow or orange sponge growing on its shell. The sponge gradually dissolves the shell and encases the crab's abdomen protectively. Barnacles may live on the crab's mobile home, and ragworms may share the shell with the crab; one ragworm species is only ever found in the shell of a hermit crab.

Rock pools usually have sea anemones ornamenting their depths, waving their tentacles around in the hope of catching a passing meal. I think that sea anemones are among the most beautiful of all marine animals; their graceful tentacles often look like the petals of a flower. They occur in a wide range of colours, including red, purple, green and blue; some are spotted or striped.

Some sea anemones are able to move about slowly, or even swim weakly; but they usually burrow into mud or sand, or live attached to a rock or shell by their base. When disturbed, the sea anemone folds its tentacles over its mouth and contracts the upper edge of its body, so that it looks like a full draw-string bag, tightly closed.

The mouth is in the centre of the tentacles, and is the only opening in the sac-like body. The tentacles are armed with stinging cells so that, when a small sea creature swims by the sea anemone and touches a tentacle, the stinging cells explode and send out barbed or poisoned threads to impale the victim, which is rendered motionless and is swept into the captor's mouth.

The red beadlet anemone, which is very common in rock pools, is quite an aggressive animal. If, while waving its tentacles around for food, one beadlet anemone touches another, they begin to fight. They tuck their tentacles in and sway away from each other, then, suddenly, one of them will swing towards its opponent, stinging for all it is worth. The defeated

Sea anemones contract to a rounded, flat-topped mass of firm jelly when the tide is out. When beneath the sea, the animal extends its tentacles which sting passing prey.

anemone sometimes becomes detached after this onslaught, and it will certainly move to another area.

Sea anemones are very resilient; they withstand the hazards of being stranded by the tide, when the temperature may be very high or very low with a frost. An exposed sea anemone faces the danger of having to withstand the effect of sun and wind together, which may dry the creature out. These problems are usually solved by the anemones retracting their tentacles and closing their mouths, then waiting for the next high tide.

Sea anemones expand their colourful tentacles to capture prey. Here you can see a dahlia anemone on the top left; a snake locks anemone, bottom left; in the centre there is a strawberry anemone; on the bottom right a gem anemone and the three above on the right are beadlet anemones.

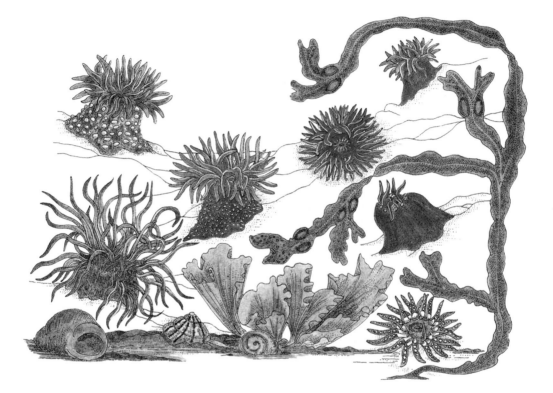

STRANDED

I expect there are a lot of people like me, who walk along the high tide line looking to see what the sea has brought in – besides old flip-flops and plastic bottles.

There are two kinds of 'mermaids' purses' to spot. These are the egg cases, usually empty, of dogfish and skates (rays); they are flat, tough, oblong and dark coloured, with tendrils extending from each corner.

Skates are flat fish with tough leathery skins rather than scales; the eyes are on top of the body and the mouth is underneath. Most skates feed on bottom-living animals such as smaller flat fish, sand eels and crabs which they hunt down by means of a well-developed sense of smell.

The common skate & its 'mermaid's purse' egg case, which has a hooked horn at each corner. Sticky hairs may be present on the 'purse'.

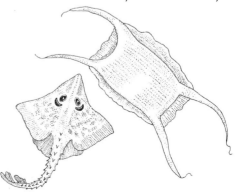

A female skate produces a small number of large eggs, and each egg is contained inside the protective envelope we know as a 'mermaid's purse'. The eggs in their cases are usually laid in shallow water, anchored to stones or large shells by their tapered corners. It takes up to fifteen months for an egg to incubate, and a long time for the little fish to mature; because of this, and because so few eggs are produced, the skate population is declining as fishing pressures increase.

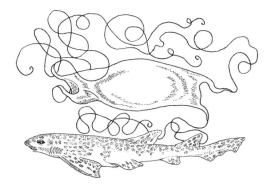

The egg case of the lesser spotted dog fish or rock salmon, has long tendrils extending from each corner.

The dogfish, or rock salmon, has a similar egg pouch to the skate, but it is lighter coloured and a little longer, and has long tendrils extending from each corner by which it is fastened to seaweed when it is newly laid.

You may find the egg ribbons of sea lemons and the egg strings of sea hares in the flotsam and jetsam of the tide line. Sea lemons and sea hares are two species of sea slug; sea slugs are related to winkles and whelks, as well as to garden slugs and snails. They are carnivores and graze on small animals attached to the sea bed – where the sea slug crawls around on a foot, for all the world like a garden slug. One big difference is that sea slugs do not usually have a shell – not even a tiny one as garden slugs do – so the gills that they breathe through are displayed on the body in various patterns, according to the species.

The animals themselves are often brightly coloured and include some of the most beautiful creatures you will find in coastal waters. Sea slugs come inshore to spawn, and then they die. They are, like garden slugs, hermaphrodites, possessing both male and female sex organs; this means that any individual of a species can mate with any other individual of that species, so allowing every single animal to produce eggs. The reproductive organs are on the right-hand side of the body, and during mating the animals pair in a head-to-tail position with their right sides together. Each sea slug passes sperm to the other and these are stored until the eggs are laid. Laying the eggs is a long business; the animal chooses a suitable site, then slowly moves round in circles, leaving a spiral coil of eggs in a neat characteristic pattern.

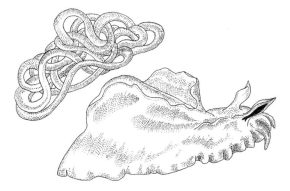

The sea hare has a very thin shell & it is a link between snails & true sea slugs. Long strings of orange-pink eggs are laid around seaweed.

The eggs hatch into tiny larvae, which drift with the tidal currents for weeks before sinking to the sea bed to search for food. Sea slugs are very particular feeders, and only the larvae who find the correct food will develop further; so, from the tens of thousands of eggs produced, only a very small proportion will settle near the diet which is suitable for them to live on.

You may also find the eggs of the necklace shell, another carnivorous gastropod. These eggs are wound spirally into collars of jelly with embedded sand grains.

156

The necklace-shaped egg mass has a honeycomb pattern and each cell is an egg capsule. The snail-like animal that belongs inside the necklace shell, *Natica alderi*, has a comparatively large foot which expands over part of the shell when the animal is active. You may find its track on undisturbed sand, but don't be surprised if suddenly the track disappears and the animal, too; it will have burrowed into the sand to hunt for its prey of cockles.

Pale yellow or grey rounded lumps, looking like pieces from coarse bathroom sponges, will probably be the empty egg cases of the common whelk. The whelk lays a great number of eggs in coils to form a spherical mass; usually the egg cases are empty when you find them. The young develop fully inside the egg cases, and hatch out when they are ready to lead an independent life.

Flat, oval, white 'bones' are often washed up on the shore; these are up to 18 cm (7 in) long and 1 cm (½ in) thick in the centre. This structure forms the internal skeleton of the cuttlefish; it is a porous 'bone' which in life is filled with gas to form a buoyancy organ, regulating the vertical position of the cuttlefish in the water.

The common cuttlefish is up to 30 cm (1 ft) long. It has an oval body which is dark brown, striped or mottled above and pale below, but the animal is able to change colour quite quickly to blend in with its background. The mouth is surrounded by ten tentacles, of which two are usually longer than the others, and can be extended or retracted as the cuttlefish hunts its prey of small fish and swimming crustaceans.

Cuttlefish have large brains, so are relatively intelligent and capable of learning by experience. Sometimes their eggs are washed up with the seaweed fronds to which they are anchored; the eggs hang like bunches of small pointed grapes.

If you are very lucky you may find a bean; these drift to some coasts with the Gulf Stream. There are two species which have often been found. *Mucuna urens* is a bean from tropical America; it is dark purple-brown with a black rim bordered with light brown. The other tropical bean, *Entada gigas*, is a shiny brown, broad-bean-shaped pulse from the West Indies. In some places these beans are called 'Marybeans' after the Virgin Mary, because they are thought to bring the finder good fortune. I don't know about that, but I felt lucky when I found mine.

It is always exciting to discover a fossil among the pebbles and shells left behind by the sea. When we lived on the Welsh coast we were very fortunate to find a pool which was formed in the rock in which an ammonite had left the elaborately decorated pattern of its coiled shell.

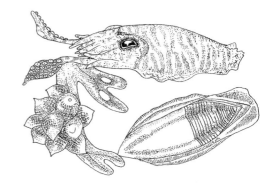

The internal, porous cuttlefish shell strengthens the animal's body & provides it with buoyancy. The black eggs are known as sea raisins or sea grapes.

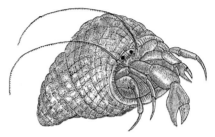

The hermit crab's soft body is hidden in the empty shell of another animal.

THE LANDWARD SIDE

Inland from the tide line, the coast has several distinct habitats; there may be towering cliffs, sandy, muddy or shingly strands never washed by the sea, or sand dunes or dune slacks with fascinating life webs of their own.

Each habitat has its own distinct and specialized plant life that is adapted to life by the sea, where there is more salt in the environment than many plants can bear.

Imagine how difficult it must be for plants to live on a shingly strand, where there is no shelter from wind or spray carried by the wind. The pebbles hold little or no water and are unstable, so plants growing there have to anchor themselves down with long roots; these roots are also able to reach water under the pebbles.

Here you may find the yellow horned poppy, with its curved seed pod of up to 30 cm (1 ft) long; cabbage-like clumps of sea kale, whose shoots were once eaten; scented may-weed's white daisy-like flowers; and prickly blue sea holly. Where there is a little more soil, look for sea campion, with its white flowers and large bladder-like calyx; thrift, the sea pink, growing in pincushion-like mounds; and yellow bird's foot trefoil, often festooned with the yellow and black caterpillars of a six-spotted burnet moth.

I could go on and on about the networks of plants and animal life you can find on the landward side of the shore, where the dunes, cliffs, salt marshes and estuaries offer a rich and fascinating variety. However, I find the life to be found in the tidal zones so interesting that I have limited myself to those areas only; to include everything else would be a book in itself.

Look carefully at the things about you, wherever you are and wherever you go. One day you are sure to see some plant or animal that is extra special, or you may see an animal – however small – displaying some interesting behaviour pattern. You may never have the same opportunity again.

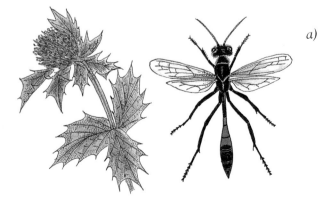
a)

a) Sea holly grows on sandy or shingly beaches. Red-banded sand wasps can be seen in areas where there are sand dunes.

b) Sea campion grows on cliffs and on shingly beaches. Shore sexton beetles, Necrodes littoralis, can often be found among the seaweeds of the upper shore.

c) Bird's foot trefoil grows in dry places; it is one of the food plants of the six-spot burnet caterpillar. The moth is day-flying and often seen by the sea.

Index